go forward, support!
the rugby of life

go forward, support!
the rugby of life

rosemary a. schmidt

GAINLINE

watertown, massachusetts

Published by Gainline Press
Watertown, Massachusetts
Copyright © 2004 by Rosemary A. Schmidt
All rights reserved, including the right of reproduction
in whole or in part, in any form.
First Edition, revised, 2003

Library of Congress Control Number 2003115427

ISBN 0-9708528-1-9

Printed in the United States of America
Printer: King Printing
Cover Photo taken by CJ Vosk © 1991
Interior Photos & Poems by Rosemary A. Schmidt © 2004
Cover Design by Jenny Boone

GAINLINE® is a registered trademark of Gainline Press

Disclaimer: The purpose of this book is to entertain and inform readers on the subject matter covered. The author and Gainline Press shall have neither liability nor responsibility to any person or entity with respect to any loss, injury, death, or damage to be caused, directly or indirectly, by the information contained in this book.

Rugby is a recreational sport with inherent risks similar to or greater than other contact sports. Suitable medical coverage (certified athletic trainer, emergency medical technician, and an on-site ambulance) is not guaranteed or required at any match or practice. Readers, players, and the parents of players under age 21, are hereby warned that qualified medical personnel are not always present at every match, and seldom at practices. If a player (or parent) is uncomfortable with playing a contact sport without the guarantee of medical coverage, then the player (or parent) should strongly reconsider their (or their child's) involvement in rugby.

Furthermore, even with appropriate medical coverage, it is possible for players to sustain serious, debilitating, life-threatening, and even life-ending injuries, as a result of playing rugby. People have died from playing rugby. It is up to the individual, or the individual's parent, to weigh the risks and benefits of playing rugby. The decision to play shall be made strictly by the individual (or parent, if player is under 21), and no liability or responsibility by the author or publisher shall be construed.

If you do not wish to be bound by the above, you may return this book to the publisher for a full refund.

Credits

All attempts to identify the originator of the dog and potato chip joke proved unsuccessful. Gratefully acknowledge their contribution to the work.

Marita Gootee quote (art and ego) gratefully reprinted with her permission.

Letter from Mom gratefully reprinted with her permission.

Jo Rutkowski quote on back cover gratefully reprinted with her permission.

Excerpt from "Women play a rugged game," by Susan Bickelhaupt, *The Boston Globe*, May 26, 1986. Reprinted courtesy of *The Boston Globe*.

Richard Ashfield quote on back cover reprinted with his permission.

Fred Paoli quote on back cover reprinted with his permission.

Cover photo gratefully reprinted with the permission of the photographer, CJ Vosk © 1991, and the players who appear in it: Morgan Whitehead, Kathy Flores, Patty Connell, Anne Flavin, MA Sorenson, Tam Breckenridge and Val Sullivan (US); and Jane Mitchell and Sam Robson (England).

Rugby and soccer history condensed from the following web pages:
www.rfu.com
www.soccerpulse.com
www.geocities.com/sissio/SOCCERHIST.html
www.geocities.com/tomokomatsui2002/history.html

Lyric Credits

go forward, support!
the rugby of life

dedication

To my Dad, who taught me to believe in myself.

To the memory of my Uncle Bill who gave me my first tennis racquet, because if he hadn't, I probably would never have gone out for the tennis team, and then I surely would not have joined the basketball and track teams, and would never have considered playing rugby, and I wouldn't be the same person I am today. Never underestimate the power of a single kind act, especially in the life of a child.

To all the ruggers from the University of Illinois and Beantown and everywhere in between: Thank you. You've been the greatest teachers of all. This book is for you.

rs

For the love of our players, coaches, and supporters – past, present, and future – and for the love of our sport.

Beantown

Contents

Poetic Interludes

Photographs

Recipes

foreword

Rose and I first crossed paths by phone. She was in the Greater Boston area for the foreseeable future and called our rugby house in the summer of 1991 looking for fellow Midwesterner Lisa Gartner. As fate would have it, Lisa was back in Chicago for a stretch, so Rose was stuck talking to me. Shortly afterwards, Rose ended up ditching the downtown B & B where she was staying and spent the summer in our rugby household. And, well, we've been friends ever since.

Five years later, on a rainy Saturday in June, a FedEx truck pulled up in front of my house. As long as you're not under surveillance, having a FedEx truck turn up at your house is a moment full of possibilities. Who? What? For me?? The package contained the first manuscript; 96 loose pages of Rose's yet unnamed book. I'm glad it was raining that Saturday because it was perfect reading weather and the book was delightful. Real laugh out loud moments intertwined with reflective passages that make you think about your life, your experiences, your effect on other people, and your contributions. Personally, I also enjoyed reliving several *I was there* moments like "what's your job?" and Kerry Kilander stepping up to the plate back in 1996.

I've tracked the progress of this book from that rainy Saturday to today. Along the way I had many interesting conversations with Rose on topics I knew nothing about, such as cover art, permission fees, and the significance and consequence of spine widths.

I'll tell you what I do know – my friend Rose is a Renaissance woman – she's no armchair rugger or philosopher, she's the real deal – athlete, artist, poet, philosopher, traveler, writer, photographer, and friend.

What Rose shares – and we already know – is that you can learn something every time you step out on either side of the touch-line. What you are open to experiencing and learning is up to you. Thanks for sharing your artful and philosophic prose on rugby and life. I learned a great deal from reading and pondering, and since the summer of 1991 I've learned a few things from being your friend.

My published commentary has been pretty limited to a few collegiate tournament write-ups in rugby rags. I was given the honor of writing this foreword and while the task was slightly daunting, I agreed. (I mean, this is my one shot, right?) Now that I do understand the impact of the foreword word count on the spine width and subsequently, the cover art, I think I'll stop here.

In closing, thank God serendipity smiles on a rainy day, Rose, and thanks too, for including me in your creative process. It's been a most enjoyable ride.

Mary Dixey
Beantown RFC

introduction

Is not the point of introducing a work to put forth prelimi-
nary comments crafted to encourage the reader to go ahead, take the
plunge, and read the book? My dilemma as I put pen to paper was
this: I knew nothing about rugby other than what I had learned by
reading Ms. Schmidt's book. I was wholly unqualified to frame this
text within a meaningful historical or cultural context.

Perhaps, I thought, it would be better to introduce the
author, rosemary a. schmidt, and then ease into her work. The problem was, I had not seen Rose but once since our grade school days,
some 30 years ago.

I finally decided to follow the clichéd advice all writers carry
around: "Write what you know." Accordingly, I resolved to introduce
the person with whom I *am* quite familiar – Rose, a small, skinny kid
in a blue plaid uniform. Long ago, we had been best friends at Our
Lady of Good Counsel, an elementary school on the scruffy side of a
blue-collar community one hour due west of Chicago. We were the
kind of friends who resembled introverted twins in their own little
world. As the other girls played hopscotch and dolls, we withdrew to
write a newspaper and invent our own language.

Generally, the nuns indulged our creative streak. For example, they allowed us to present our book reports on our home-made
TV, which we lugged to school on the back of a wagon. The set was a
cardboard box decorated with construction paper and aluminum foil
knobs. The screen was a cut-out square through which we scrolled
miles of meticulously illustrated shelf paper. The voice-overs from
behind the box helped our otherwise dull reports magically come to
life.

As for sports, we had no interest back then, especially in the
activity that passed for girls' athletics, namely cheerleading. Perhaps

we were too young. I do remember the sting of being second-to-last picked for P.E. teams. I was grateful to Rose for using her influence to make sure I wasn't last on board.

Years later, Rose sent me a note out of the blue, or out of "left field," as she put it. She was planning to videotape a rugby game near my home, outside of Washington, D.C., and wanted to know if I would be interested in reconnecting. Of course! She stayed over, entertaining my children with cool, but improbable stories about a wild game called rugby.

The next day, Rose and I drove to the game with my young son, arriving in time to see an ambulance remove a player from the field. The game quickly resumed, at full throttle, as if nothing had happened. It was then that Rose explained to us that part of the appeal of rugby for her was that, just like in real life, there are no timeouts. Play is continuous. You just deal with things as they come.

I asked Rose how *she* had ever managed to make the college team, what with her petite frame and cautious demeanor. Turns out that people choose rugby – not the other way around. There are no tryouts. Conversely, each player decides when to retire. No one throws them out. That concept alone is worthy of a chapter by a former rugby player. On that note, I cordially invite you to proceed straight ahead…

Lisa Jo Finstrom

preface

I started playing rugby in 1986, while in graduate school at the University of Illinois at Urbana-Champaign. It was my second year, I needed something to do, and I would have done Tae Kwon Do if I hadn't been broke at the time. But I was broke, so I joined the rugby club instead. And things haven't been the same since. I had never played such a sport before. I'd never tackled anyone before, not even in "touch" football. Not only did I find out that I could tackle, but that it was fun, and intensely satisfying. It was different from all the other sports I had ever played – track, softball, and tennis. Rugby is far more visceral. It's all-out effort until the last whistle blows. It's you, your teammates, the opponents, the field, the ref, and the ball. It's not tidy, it's real-time running clock do-or-die commitment. The intensity of the game is matched only by the revelry of the rugby party. It is a time-honored tradition for the home team to host the drink up. Mud, blood, sweat, and beers.

In 1992, I moved to Boston and joined up with Beantown Rugby Football Club. Having played rugby at different levels (college vs. club) and in different regions of the country (Midwest vs. New England), I have found the players to have a universal passion for this sport, whether they play for Beantown or Berkeley, Mizzou or FSU (University of Missouri, Florida State University). When you play rugby, it's as though you've been adopted into a rather large, extended family. There are more than 400 women's rugby teams (college and city clubs) in the United States.

This isn't a how-to-play-rugby book; it's not an everybody-*should*-play-rugby book. Rugby simply opened my eyes to a passion that I've tried to apply to the rest of my life. In many ways, life is a lot like rugby. No timeouts. No protection from the elements. No free substitutions. You run, you fall, and you get back up. The rules are always changing. And it's not always fair. The referee doesn't always see everything. Sure, it's a game, but the only way to play that game is as though it matters. Yes, you may get hurt if you play, but that's the chance you take. You'll never lose if you don't play, but you'll never win either. It's about taking risks, and letting things matter, while remembering how little most things in this life really do matter, outside of loving well, living honorably, being there for each other, trying to do what is right, and being thankful for the gifts in our lives. The only things that are matters of life or death are, in fact, life and death.

This book has been my own personal *Shawshank Redemption*, a testament to what can be accomplished by just chipping away – one day, one sentence, one paragraph, or one chapter – at a time. Before starting this endeavor, I enjoyed reading two very different books: *If You Want To Write*, by Brenda Ueland, and *I'm Good Enough, I'm Smart Enough, and Doggone It, People Like Me!* by Stuart Smalley (really Al Franken). Both of these books, in their own way, provided great inspiration to me, and I highly recommend them to you. While I never took to my bed for days with packages of cookies, I still often identified with the character, Stuart Smalley, and cannot deny occasionally using Milano's cookies as a reward, at one point curling up in the fetal position on the floor of my office, or suffering any number of nervous conditions. I've been nervous, I've been a wreck, I've been the proverbial nervous wreck. But Stuart Smalley made me laugh, and helped me see the humor of my own situation. Unlike Stuart's book, this is not a book of affirmations. The only thing I can affirm is that we're all human, and thus susceptible to all the attendant joys and cruelties of this condition.

Brenda Ueland brought another message: "Everybody is talented, original, and has something important to say." And it's usually worth taking the time to listen. In fact, Brenda Ueland wrote that it is "the only way to love a person… by listening to them and seeing and believing in the god, in the poet, in them. For by doing this, you keep the god and poet alive and make it flourish." To see and believe in the god and poet in each of us. What a simply beautiful message.

And so, I thank all the people who encouraged me and had some part in bringing this project to fruition. Thanks to the crew who physically contributed to making this project a reality:

Editor: Chris Casatelli
Cover Designer: Jenny Boone
Cover Photo: CJ Vosk
Photographic Printing Services: Newtonville Camera
Printer: the whole team at King Printing, Lowell, MA

Thank you to the many wonderful and helpful people I came in contact with while seeking permission to reprint the various quotes herein, and especially the very kind folks at Hal Leonard, Warner Brothers, the *Vancouver Sun*, *The Boston Globe*, Graywolf Press, Harvard University Press, and The Albert Einstein Archives.

Many thanks also go out to Ed Hagerty at *Rugby Magazine* and Ross Hamilton at the Rugby Museum for sharing their knowledge of the game. And, thank you Beantown – you have taught me much, and taught me well.

And, going way back, thanks to the 1983 editorial staff of the University of Dayton *Flyer News* for taking a chance, and giving a column to a non-English major.

A variety of things helped spur me on in the course of this project: WPLM Easy 99.1 (ahh, so soothing), the Indigo Girls, Syd Straw, the Internal Revenue Service (see, it's not just a hobby!), the Patent and Trademark Office (thanks for the deadline!), Pepperidge Farm, Earl Grey, post-its (by the thousands), and the long, snowy New England winters, especially 1993-1994, 1995-1996, and the particularly long, protracted winter of 2003 (thank you God). And snow in April.

Thanks especially to all the unofficial reviewers who read the manuscript in its most embryonic forms, and also helped shape its evolution by sharing their feedback: my dear old friend Lisa Jo Finstrom, Mary Dixey, T (Molloy) Heck, Betsy Kimball, Patty Connell (you're a crayon in my book), Darlene Connors, Joan Morrissey, Jan Rutkowski, Walter Lyons, Lisa Gartner, Marita

go forward, support!

Gootee, Mari Brinkman, Anna Krasko, Denise Block, both Eileens (Cronin and Adams), Vicki Volz, Ellen Iorio, Jane Gronholm, Marie Wojtas, and Susan, my love – thanks for all the support and encouragement.

Thank you to all my friends and family who listened to me and believed in me, who saw the god and poet in me, even when I felt myself certainly to be neither.

rs

chapter 1
a little history

"Bring your lunch, and I'll tell you a story," as my Dad has always said. Better yet, bring me a lunch, and I'll try not to talk with my mouth full. If you are reading this, then I can safely assume one of the following:

a. you play rugby,
b. you used to play rugby,
c. you know someone who plays rugby or
    used to play rugby,
d. you are related to a rugby player,
e. you are curious about playing rugby:
    you may have only a vague awareness that the game
    exists, and may or may not have seen an actual game
    being played,
f. you are just a Renaissance person, interested in all sorts
    of cultural experiences, and want to broaden your
    horizons by learning more about rugby,
g. you bought the wrong book by mistake,
    but can't find the receipt, or
h. you received this book as a gift.

In the beginning, in many countries and cultures (China, Japan, Italy, Northern France, the Aztecs, Romans, and Greeks, to name a few), there were people playing with balls, using various means to move it across a space to score points in a variety of ways. This went on for centuries, and overall it was pretty good. In Britain, all of these ball games were known as "football," whether it was a kicking, carrying, or dribbling game. Eventually, these people playing with balls begat both rugby football and soccer (also known as

Association football), and rugby then begat football (also known as American football). And, of course, American football begat much that is wrong with American society (overpaid athletes, skewed values systems, a spectator culture of couch-potatoes, really stupid beer commercials, etc.), and yet I can't keep myself from watching it. (Go Patriots!). But I digress.

It is not clear exactly when the primordial foot-ball game was first introduced to Britain, but this island would be responsible for giving birth to both rugby and soccer. It has been speculated that its roots may go back as early as the 3rd century AD, or as recent as the 11th century AD, perhaps related to the Norman Conquest of 1066.

The early ball games here varied widely, depending on the local rules of the village, the ball, and the playing field available. Games were played in the streets and in open fields. The ball took various forms, but was often constructed of leather, and filled with any number of things (rags, hair, feathers, straw, fur, etc.) to make it durable enough to withstand the abuse it took during the game. The rules varied widely from village to village, but generally it was a very rag-tag game, where practically anything might be allowed, depending on local custom, except perhaps for outright murder. Fatalities were always a possible outcome, though.

The ball was often moved forward using the feet, either kicking or dribbling it, and handling of the ball was also allowed under certain conditions. Kicking was typically allowed, but was of varying utility, depending on the ball's construction. Imagine trying to kick a bean bag chair.

The foot-ball games went through various stages of acceptance and criticism with the changing cultural tides. At some points it was decried as a waste of time, taking young men's time away from more practical skills such as archery, a staple exercise in preparing the common man for war. As a form of public entertainment, it was denounced by the Puritan movement of the 16th century. At certain points, it was even banned by the monarchy in England and Scotland. Separate from these complaints based on principle, the games frequently led to substantial property damage as the mob-like crowds played through a town. They disturbed the peace. Despite these attacks, though, the foot-ball games endured, thanks to the people's love of the game.

The advent of public schools in the early 19th century would profoundly change the perception and development of these ball-games. The schools needed to provide recreation for the students, and these foot-ball games filled the bill perfectly: minimal equipment was needed, and the game engaged large numbers of players within a small area. Some ground rules were observed, but each individual school still maintained its own unique set of rules.

Foot-ball games became a part of life at the many public schools. One of these was Rugby School, in the town of Rugby, Warwickshire, England. Founded in 1567, the school moved to a new site in 1750 with a large two-acre grounds for physical recreation. The schoolmasters did not organize or supervise sports for the boys, but they kept an eye on them, to make sure they didn't cause any trouble.

The early rules of the game at Rugby School were quite fluid, and constantly under evaluation and subject to change. The schoolboys would meet after each game, to discuss the rules and how they affected the play. If they liked a rule, they kept it. If they didn't like a rule, they dropped it. And new rules could always be added. The games were played on a grass field on the school grounds. In fact, these same fields are still used for rugby today. They played with a bladder-shaped ball that derived its shape from the fact that it was literally constructed of a pig's bladder enclosed within a leather covering. While we speak of a pig's skin in American football, we should really be referring to a pig's bladder in rugby! Doesn't have quite the same ring, though, does it? Let's just call it a rugby ball.

In the time period of interest, the game at Rugby School was played primarily with the feet. Handling the ball was forbidden, with one exception. If the ball was in mid-air, it could be caught. At this point, everyone would freeze where they were, including the ball catcher. The catcher could back up a distance from where he caught the ball, and then either kick it downfield, or place the ball on the ground and attempt a kick through the goalposts for a goal. Everyone else could not move until the ball catcher had moved past the point where he had originally caught the ball.

It was 1823 and – as the story goes – some fellows were playing their local brand of foot-ball when something different happened. One of the players, a 16-year old by the name of William Webb Ellis, caught the ball. He did not retreat, nor did he kick it. He did the unthinkable. He ran forward with the ball in his hands. There's no record of what happened next, but I suspect that his opponents probably reacted by doing only the next natural and logical thing: they probably tried to tackle him. And thus, the sport of rugby was born.

At least that's how the story goes. There is actually very little in the way of concrete evidence of this event to substantiate the William Webb Ellis story. Records show that he attended Rugby School in that timeframe, but there is no written record of his first ball-carry until more than 50 years after the event, and no eye-witness accounts. All we have is the word of a former Rugby School boy, Mathew Bloxom, who mentioned William Webb Ellis in a reply to the Old Rugby Boys Society, as they were doing some research into the origins of the game. Bloxom was the only respondent to mention Ellis, and in fact admitted that he was not even a schoolboy at the time, and had only heard about the event from a friend. It is known that, some fifteen years later, another Rugby School boy, named Jem Mackie, had popularized the carrying game through his prowess at it, and by 1838 "running in" had become the accepted method of scoring at Rugby School.

Maybe the William Webb Ellis story is true, but was passed down only through oral accounts. And, maybe the story sprang out of a keen desire to pin-point rugby's beginnings. No one is sure why William Webb Ellis became the Founding Father of Rugby. Was it a revolutionary act of one individual, or the evolutionary process of a group over time? And perhaps something more was involved.

The Old Rugbeans were researching the origins of rugby in 1895, at a time when the sport was going through major changes. That was the year the game split in two, with the formation of the Northern Union (later to be known as Rugby League), composed primarily of working class players. The clubs that stayed in the Rugby Football Union (RFU) were made up of middle class players, most of whom had attended public school. It has been speculated that William Webb Ellis was elevated to this status by the RFU to demonstrate the middle class' exclusive claim to the game. (For more on this, read *Rugby's Great Split*, by Tony Collins.)

And then again, maybe it was just poor record-keeping, and the frailties of human memory and the oral tradition. Why was America named for Amerigo Vespucci and not Christopher Columbus? History is full of such riddles.

In any case, ball-carrying was officially sanctioned in the Rugby School rules in 1845, with the first set of published foot-ball rules. When Rugby School boys left to go to University or work, they brought their style of foot-ball with them. New clubs, playing the Rugby-style of foot-ball, sprang up throughout the country. (For more information on the early game at Rugby School, read the book, *Running with the Ball*, by Jenny Macrory.)

The official split between rugby and soccer came several years later. In 1863, the Football Association was founded in an effort to develop one set of foot-ball laws. The Association wanted to outlaw some of the rougher tactics, such as shin-kicking, tripping, etc. One player from the Blackheath Rugby Club, F.W. Campbell, voiced his dismay over the Association's approach to the laws, saying it would destroy the game and eliminate all interest in it. Blackheath left the Football Association as a result, and effectively took the ball-carrying game with them.

As it turned out, those members who were against the rougher tactics also disapproved of carrying the ball. This group wound up being the majority voice, and thus soccer was born.

It's obvious how rugby got it's name, but where did soccer come from? Sock her? No, ladies didn't play rugby or soccer yet. A fellow named Charles Wreford Brown coined the term from the root word, association.

The ball-carrying rugby-style game did not disappear, obviously, otherwise the story would end right here. Rather, a push was made to standardize the rules of rugby in 1870, and representatives from 22 clubs and schools met in January 1871, giving rise to the English Rugby Football Union and the first (but not last) set of rugby laws. The first international match was played that year between England and Scotland. And, ironically enough, laws prohibiting tripping and shin kicking were eventually enacted, with Blackheath being one of the most vocal supporters.

As more people became interested in the game, the sport quickly caught on throughout the United Kingdom and spread to various corners of the world, thanks in part to colonialism and later the effects of globalization. The first rugby game in the United States was played between Harvard University and McGill University in 1874. American football would take shape around the turn of the century, first with the addition of downs, and later the forward pass.

There are many, many more details about how rugby has evolved since that (alleged) fateful day in 1823, but this chapter is called "a little history," not "a lot of history." Whether man or myth, the concept of William Webb Ellis still stands as a symbol of what can happen when people question the rules, take a risk, and try something completely different.

In a nutshell (or a pig's bladder), this is how it all started.

chapter 2
the accidental rugger

Everyone who plays rugby has their own story of how they came to the game. In the US, it is often by chance or accident that someone gets mixed up with a rugby club. It's clearly very different in the major rugby-playing nations, where rugby is a huge part of the day-to-day culture. Rugby is as popular in these countries as the NFL is here in the US. Kids may start playing touch rugby in grammar school. They grow up watching rugby, going to rugby games, and just in general having a good sense of what rugby is all about. They actually have a general idea of the rules before they start playing.

This may not sound all that remarkable, but when I started playing, it wasn't that uncommon for the first rugby game that someone played in, to also be the first rugby game they had ever seen. That was the case for me. There are also plenty of stories of innocent spectators being convinced to play minutes before the game, if a team showed up short-handed. At least I had been going to rugby practice before playing that first game.

The only problem was that I'd joined the team in the spring season, which meant the majority of the practices were held inside the armory building because the field was still too frozen, snow covered, or wet to play on. This also meant we couldn't really do any tackling or other rough and tumble stuff that involved lying or falling on the ground, which covers much of what is done in rugby. As a result, we were limited to doing a lot of running around and a bunch of unusual drills. To the uninitiated, these were very unusual drills. Take this ball, run into that player (but not so fast that you fall), turn your back to that player, and then a couple of other players will come up behind you and throw their arms over you. Taken out of context, these drills felt more like folk dancing class. Or the hokey-pokey. The other problem was that we didn't have enough players to simulate opposition very well. ("Run with the ball up to the orange traffic cone, pretend to encounter opposition and pass the ball out…")

If the practice drills seemed funny, the actual games were even more confusing. This wasn't the first time that this had ever happened to me, though. When I started high school, I decided that I'd like to go out for the tennis team. All summer, I had been playing tennis with my cousin, Joe, out on the street where we lived, and I thought that I had gotten pretty good. Of course, when I showed up to practice, and the coach sent me out to play Linda down on court five, and it came time for the first serve… Well, how was I supposed to know that the serve was supposed to land in some little box?

"Out? What do you mean out? It went over the net." There weren't any lines on Talma Street, and certainly no service boxes. "In" and "out" were defined by curbs and parked cars. What a nutty game. But I stuck it out. I loved tennis, and the solid "thwack" of the ball coming off the racquet. And I ultimately surprised people, including myself. If I had gone to a big high school where they'd had cuts, I probably would have been cut my freshman year, if not laughed off the courts. Instead, by my senior year, I was captain of the team. We weren't stellar, but we were very good. More importantly, we gave it our best effort and we were a close-knit team.

It could have been worse. A friend of mine, who shall remain nameless, went out for cross-country skiing when she started high school. She thought it was odd that they spent so much time running at practice. And then she thought they were really nuts when the first meet was scheduled and they didn't even have any snow on the ground yet. When she brought this up to the coach during practice, everybody just laughed. They thought she was joking. So, it was when she showed up to the first meet that she discovered that she had inadvertently joined the cross-country *running* team! Well, what else could she do? She ran cross-country. Of course she went on to play rugby.

Well, rugby is *way* nuttier than tennis or cross-country, the running or skiing variety. I realized this even before the first indoor practice at the armory. I decided this when I walked into the rugby meeting at the student union, and thought I overheard some players saying that I looked like I could be a good hooker. Excuse me? Of course, I came to find out that a hooker is the name of one of the positions in the front row of the scrum. The hooker tries to "hook" the ball back with her foot, so that it comes out to her team's side. We'll discuss scrums later. The sport is rife with all kinds of British terms, for obvious reasons.

So, I was sitting there in the meeting, and they were going over what one needs to play rugby. Rugby jerseys were provided. What a relief! Part of why I'd gone to the rugby meeting instead of doing Tae Kwon Do with my roommates was that I was broke. I didn't have the $20 fee for the Tae Kwon Do class. As it turned out, rugby dues were also $20 per season, but the club had an easy payment plan.

So, the list went on. Mouth guard, cleats, rugby socks, rugby shorts… Rugby shorts! Special shorts for rugby? Why couldn't I just wear some other pair of navy blue shorts that I already had? The answer: regular shorts would probably get ripped apart in the very first game. In rugby, the kit (uniform) is part of the game. When Ellis or Mackie went running with the ball, the guys on the other team probably tried to stop him, by grabbing him by whatever they could get their hands on: shirt, shorts, whatever. The invention of rugby jerseys and rugby shorts probably ensued shortly after tackling was introduced to the game. The rugby shorts are made to be very durable, with all the seams reinforced and stitched about 47 times. I've even had my rugby shorts get ripped, though. But not along the seams.

A side note on rugby jerseys: you should have one. Even if you never play rugby, never set foot on a rugby pitch (field) or see a game being played, you should still get yourself a rugby jersey. Just because it feels good. And it's a fashion statement. There's something about a rugby jersey – the look, the feel of the tightly woven cotton and crisp collar. There are newer, quick-drying polyester jerseys available now, but it just doesn't seem right to be wearing polyester in a rugby game. I much prefer the old cotton jerseys. You feel tough, just putting one on. It makes you feel like you could tackle someone.

chapter 3
some rugby nuts and bolts

How did this game develop after that fateful day when Ellis (allegedly) picked up the ball and ran? Like I said, his teammates probably tried to tackle him. That's my guess. Maybe the second time one of the guys ran with the ball, he passed it off before he got tackled. If he did, that pass would have been a lateral one. The offside rules are somewhat similar to those in soccer, not surprising given their common origin, having some pretty profound effects on how the game of rugby is played. Forward passes are not allowed. Blocking also is not allowed. In fact, it's called obstruction, and it will earn you a penalty. If you are downfield of the ball, you are most likely offside, and possibly obstructing. You're also essentially useless to your team, since you're not allowed to receive a pass or field a kick from an offside position.

Poetic Interlude #1
(the first of many)

Claire!
Claire!
You're useless there!

This is an actual quote from an actual rugby player (who shall remain nameless), made during an actual rugby game which took place somewhere in the Midwest sometime in the mid-1980s. Claire was offside in a big way, and one of her teammates was informing her of this fact. Poor Claire! It was her first season. She did catch on, though, and managed to redeem herself. By the end of the season, she was making some pretty amazing runs with the ball, surprising quite a few people, including herself. (Note: In order to preserve the poetry of the Poetic Interlude, Claire's name has *not* been changed.)

Since lateral passes are the rule of the day, to be of any use, you must come from behind the player with the ball. When the ball carrier meets opposition, she has the option of passing the ball off to the next player running up in the line. And the next ball carrier could do the same, and so on. If life were simple and perfect, that would be it. Run and pass, run and pass, run and pass until someone scores a try (like a touchdown, but worth five points, and you must literally touch the ball down to the ground). But, people get tackled, passes get missed, and things get messy. The proverbial shit happens.

In American football, a whistle would blow, and everybody would get in a huddle, chitchat about the next play, wait for some guys to take some measurements, check the replay, maybe make some substitutions, or even take a timeout. For a commercial, no less. Not so in rugby. The continuous play aspect of the earliest forms of the foot-ball games was also carried over to both rugby and soccer. So, what happens when the ball carrier gets tackled? The ball carrier must release the ball, and make it available to other players. It's the law. (No rules in this sport, just laws.) And when the ball is made available, anyone can pick it up and run with it. As a result, there's not much time to gloat or gloom about the last play. You always have to be looking for the next play, and figuring out where you need to be, so that you can be useful.

Remember that the ball is essentially the line of scrimmage, and determines who is offside or onside (naughty or nice). To be of any use, you need to be coming from an onside position – from behind the ball. If you're downfield, you have to retreat until you're behind the ball before you can join in the reindeer games.

After a tackle, and the ball is made available, and it's just sitting there, a lot of things can and do happen. If you come upon a ball like this, you mainly have two choices: pick up the ball (maul) or leave it on the ground (ruck). If you pick up the ball, you may sprint off, but more likely than not, you'll run into some opposition. Yet, you want to protect the ball and keep it on your side. Hopefully, your teammates aren't far behind you, and will soon be there to bind onto you, using a full arm and shoulder to grab hold over you, to protect the ball from the opposing players, and continue the drive forward. The idea is to create a wall or wedge of people between the ball and the opposition. At the same time, the opposing players are also plowing into this thing from the opposite side, trying to push it in the opposite direction. This thing is called a maul. ("A woman's place is in the maul.") Mauls can get messy, though, with a lot of hands on the ball. And if the ball gets hung up, and doesn't come out, then the ref will blow the whistle and call for a scrum (to be discussed later).

The other option is the ruck. Instead of picking up the ball, especially when the opposition is right there, you can grab and bind on to the opposing player over the ball. More players from both sides can join in. The idea is to drive the opposition backwards over the ball, so the ball comes out the back side of the ruck to your team's side.

A ruck often produces a faster, cleaner ball out, since the ball is never picked up, and is therefore less likely to get hung up with half a dozen hands on it, as so often happens in a maul. A maul can become a ruck, if the ball gets placed to the ground during the fracas. But a ruck can-not-ever-really *ever* become a maul, because once the ball is on the ground and a ruck is formed, it's illegal to use your hands to move the ball. The technical term for this is "hands in the ruck," or "hands in" for short. If the referee sees somebody doing this, the whistle will blow and a penalty will be charged to the offending team.

The whole point of rucks and mauls is to keep the game flowing, with minimal interruptions of the whistle. Somehow, I've gotten this far, but haven't yet mentioned the referee. There is a referee, a whistle, and 15 of us, and 15 of them.

The referee can be a very big part of the game, but some of the best referees are the least noticed during a game. You may have been wondering if there were any rules in this nutty game, let alone a referee.

Technically speaking, there are no *rules*; they're called laws. They can all be found in the Law Book. And the laws change – a little bit – just about every year. It's a *dynamic* nutty game. So, while there are myriad laws that are in a constant state of flux, there is typically one referee assisted by two touch judges. (Touch means out of bounds.)

The touch judges help the ref by raising their flags when the ball goes into touch. Usually, the touch judges are just other team members. In important tournaments, the touch judges may be referees. When I was in college, the touch judges were typically bored, drunk, hung over, and/or clueless spectators or rookies.

Here's a good touch judge story. A friend of mine was touch judging a game, but she was also rooting for one of the teams. When her team got close to scoring a try, she got so excited that she forgot what she was doing and started cheering, waving her touch flag around in the process. The ref saw the flag go up, and blew the whistle, thinking that the ball had gone out of bounds, thereby stopping the play before the team could score. Oops.

The referee's chief objective is to allow the game to flow, while still maintaining control by enforcing the laws in a fair and consistent manner. Refereeing is not an exact science. Nothing gets measured exactly. For example, the referee paces off five meters when there's a five-meter scrum. Mostly, refereeing is an art. There's so much happening, and it's all happening so fast, and all at the same time. This is a game in which there are no do overs, and certainly no instant replays. The referee's call is final. It's just another part of this nutty game. You may see something, but if the referee didn't see it, it essentially didn't happen.

Here's a philosophy question for you: If you use your hands in the ruck and the referee doesn't see it, is it "hands in the ruck?" The answer is, "No, but..." No, but players from the other team may have seen it, and you may wind up with cleat marks on the backs of your hands if you keep it up. Realistically, though, the player-to-referee ratio is an important element of the game. How can one referee keep an eye on 30 slippery, surly ruggers? It's impossible. Players learn when refs can and can't see what they're doing, and let us say that they modify their behavior accordingly. Kind of like when you pull your foot off the gas pedal and start praying when you spy a state trooper in your path. Players also may learn the particular style of a given referee, and again may modify their play to attain whatever tiny advantage they can get in the process. This behavior modification is also known as playing the ref. To some extent, everybody does it, and everybody knows that everybody does it.

Committing infractions while the referee isn't looking might be called cheating, especially by an observant crowd of spectators. Some would say that it's only cheating if you get caught. But, in the larger picture, most teams would prefer to develop better physical skills, techniques, and strategies (which might just happen to include some creative re-interpretation of the laws).

chapter 4
more detailed nuts and bolts

There's been a lot of talk about the "flow" of the game, and yet, so far, it probably sounds like it has all the flow of a train wreck. Fifteen of us against fifteen of them, all fighting for one ball. With one ref.

Frankly, it *would* be a mess if all thirty players went for the ball all at the same time. It would be a massive dog pile. So, there are different positions. Each position does different things, requiring different skills, body builds, and personality types. There's a place for everybody. Every body. There are enough different positions in rugby, requiring different body shapes, sizes, strengths, and skills, that there is a place for everyone. For example, I may be small, but I'm slow. Hmmm. In a culture that values model-thin body types, it can be a revelation for some bigger-boned women that their body type would be so appreciated in rugby.

A friend was explaining rugby to a non-rugby acquaintance, and was making this same point. "There are all sorts of skills that are needed. Speed, strength, tackling, kicking...." The woman's face lit up. "You mean you get to kick people?" No, no, no. Kicking people is not a sanctioned part of the game, and has been banned now for many decades.

Generally, though, there are forwards and backs. The eight forwards, also known as the forward pack, tend to be larger and stronger, as they are responsible for fighting for possession of the ball. Forwards tend to spend a lot of their time in rucks and mauls. The six fleet-footed backs, also known as the back line, tend to be strong and speedy runners. They run with the ball more, working various plays in open-field situations. Aha! you say. This only adds up to fourteen. There are supposed to be fifteen players to a side!

The fifteenth player, who actually wears the number nine jersey, is the scrumhalf. The scrumhalf is usually counted as a back, but it's sort of a special position. It's a little bit like the quarterback position in football, except that there is no blocking in rugby. And no forward passes. Scrumhalves tend to be some of the smartest, scrappiest players on the field. When the ball comes out the back of a ruck or maul or whatever, the scrumhalf typically picks it up and passes it out to the backs. The forwards get untangled, and then follow the play, to be there in support, to take a pass, make a tackle, or join a ruck or maul. And so on, and so on, and so on.

It's time for The Car Analogy. Let's say our team is a car. The forwards would be the engine, the power, the driving force. They gain possession of the ball. The scrumhalf would be the drive shaft. Just as the drive shaft transfers power from the engine to the wheels, the scrumhalf moves the ball from the forwards to the backs, who are the wheels of our car. The backs then cruise down the field.

chapter 5
more highly technical rugby nuts and bolts

With this modest foundation of rugby knowledge, we are ready to move on to yet more advanced topics, such as the scrum. It's a forward thing. A scrum is a little bit like a face-off in hockey or a jump ball in basketball, except that there are eight of us going against eight of them, and there's a lot more contact involved. It's similar to a ruck, in that the ball is on the ground, and we're all bound onto each other. The difference is that it's a "set piece," meaning that it doesn't just happen spontaneously in the course of play, but only when the ref stops play due to a minor infraction. The most common such infraction is the "knock on," which means a forward pass, which includes any time that you drop, fumble, or toss the ball ahead of you on the field, whether you meant to do it or not. Example: You field a kickoff, the ball hits your arm (below the shoulder), and bounces forward. That's a knock on.

As mentioned previously, there's a great deal of emphasis put on keeping the game flowing. So, ideally, you don't have too many stoppages of the game. If the ref blew the whistle every time there was a knock on, there would be an awful lot of whistles and an awful lot of scrums. And, as much as forwards love scrummaging, it is exhausting work and takes its toll on their back and neck muscles. Plus, it's not in the spirit of keeping the game flowing. So, there's what's called the Advantage Law, also known as playing the advantage.

When there's a knock on, the referee watches to see if the opposing team (the team that did *not* knock the ball on) gains an advantage from the knock on. Let's say the ball bounces forward off my elbow, and a player from the other team scoops it up (the ball, not my elbow) and runs with it and scores, or at least gains some yardage. Even though I screwed up, it wound up being to the other team's advantage, and so the ref would let play go on. This is the reason that you'll hear people say, "play till you hear the whistle." When you see someone drop the ball forward, you cannot automatically assume that there will be a whistle, followed by a scrum. On top of that, different referees let play go on longer than others after a knock on, to see if an advantage will be gained. Besides, you and the referee may not be seeing the same thing in the same way. So, the best idea is to let the referee ref, and to just play until you hear the whistle.

Back to the scrum. Let's say that the whistle blows, and the referee calls for a scrum. The two forward packs face each other and assemble themselves into a certain set configuration at the mark, each side composed of two props, a hooker, two second rows (also called locks), two wing forwards (also known as flankers), and a number eight. I'm not going to try to explain where everybody's every body part goes in assembling a scrum, but here is a brief overview.

There's a front row – prop, hooker, prop – with the two locks behind them. These five players are all bound onto each other very, very tightly, and are thus known as the tight five. The other three are known as loose forwards, and bind on behind the tight five. The flankers join on either side of the scrum (next to the locks and behind the props), and the number eight joins in the back of the scrum, behind the locks. Although these three back row players are called loose, they also hold on very tightly during the scrum. When the scrum is over, though, they have the best chance to get out quickly and get involved in loose play, on the open field.

The opposing front rows (and everybody attached behind them) face each other, crouch down low, and upon the hooker's call, come together, so that the front rows' heads sort of interlock. If you're in the front row, you are basically ear-to-ear with your opponents. If you want to try to visualize a scrum, then do the old "here's the church, and here's the steeple" thing with your hands, but don't put up the steeple. Draw little faces on each of your fingertips. The people – your fingers – are the front row players. This kind of demonstrates the arching that occurs, as each front row player pushes her head up under the sternum of the player opposite her. I won't go into this much more, except to say that the scrum is mostly a driving thing, involving a lot of pushing. The mechanics are similar to those involved with doing a squat at the gym.

Well, the scrum is also a timing thing. The non-offending team gets to put the ball into the scrum, and thus has a certain advantage in knowing exactly when the ball will be coming in. The hooker gives a signal, the scrumhalf puts the ball in from the side, the hooker hooks the ball back with her foot, the ball comes out the back of the scrum (usually under the number eight), the scrumhalf picks it up, passes it out, and we're off and running again. (Side note, the scrumhalf is permitted to reach into the scrum and pull the ball out, without being called for hands in.)

It's interesting to note how elements of the scrum are retained in the American football scrimmage. Instead of the pyramid-shaped, glob-like structure of the scrum, the football players are spread out along the line of scrimmage. The hike of the ball back to the quarterback is equivalent to the hooking of the ball back to where the scrumhalf can pick it up. Timing is still key in synchronizing the line's forward motion with the snap of the ball. Things are just a little less certain in rugby, though, since controlling the put-in does not necessarily guarantee that your side will win the hook, or get the ball cleanly out of the scrum. Football is quite a bit more predictable in that possession of the ball is more clear-cut. In rugby, possession can be challenged at almost every turn.

As a result, the scrum is a mental thing. It really is about which side can work together, pull together, and push harder. It's all mental. I've seen some pretty funny combinations, and I've been in some pretty odd scrums, but it really is a matter of chemistry. And physics. If you've got everyone in your pack totally working together, and you've got a certain rhythm, and you're in sync, you can totally dominate a larger, stronger, less organized, less cohesive scrum. There's nothing better than when your scrums are going well. And, conversely, there is nothing worse than when your scrums are getting pushed backwards.

The bottom line is that the scrum is a physics-driving-timing-mental kind of thing.

Scrum between Beantown (on the left) and Berkeley during the final of the 2001 US Women's National Championship, played in Rockford, Illinois. Berkeley won, with a score of 41-11. (photo/rs)

chapter 6
Q: how do you score in rugby?
A: you try!

A great deal has been covered (although certainly not everything), but we haven't even touched on scoring, which is a fairly significant part of the game, considering that the team with the most points at the end of the game wins.

First of all, when you score, it's called a try. Not "tri." A try is worth five points, not three points, although, up until the law change in 1993, a try was worth four points. A try is awarded by the referee when a player touches the ball down in the try zone (which looks suspiciously very similar to the end zone in football). Although similar to the touchdown in football, the try has some subtle differences. It's not about crossing a plane; it's about touching the ball down. Furthermore, it's more than just touching the ball while it is on the ground in the end zone; a player must exert downward pressure on the ball in the try zone for it to count.

Ironically, a try is literally more like a "touch down" than the football touchdown. This makes some sense, given that American football evolved from rugby. As the sport started to evolve from rugby to football, the mode of scoring must have mutated, but somehow the touchdown terminology lingered on, like a vestigial tail. Technically speaking, though, the term touchdown should be tossed out for a more accurate description of what actually happens when a player scores in football. I suppose the term "crossplane" wouldn't be catchy enough.

Enough about football, though, and back to rugby. Every team has a story or two about a rookie who gets the ball and has some speed and somehow gets down into the try zone, but has never heard, or was never told (oops), or just forgot about the touching-down part of scoring a try. If you've got the ball, then you're still fair game to be tackled until you touch the ball down. You get the picture. Some ecstatic rookie is hopping around the try zone hooting about scoring, when they get totally turfed. Of course, there are about fourteen voices yelling, "Touch it down! Touch it down!" Which, to the rookie, sounds just like "Great job! Well done! We love you!" The point is, that it's not enough to get the ball across the line. You've got to touch it down. (Don't say I didn't tell you so!)

The significance of touching the ball down doesn't end there. It also determines the placement of the ball for the conversion kick afterwards (worth two points). If the player who scored the try was able to place the ball down right under the goal posts, then the kicker has a straight-on shot for the kick. If the try was made in the corner of the try zone, near the sideline, then the kicker has to work with a far more difficult angle. It is small consolation that the kicker is allowed to back up from the goal posts any distance. The conversion kick in rugby is far from a sure thing.

There are other kicks that can be made that are worth three points. When certain penalties are called, the non-offending team has the option of taking possession of the ball and running a play or kicking for post. If you're interested in knowing which certain penalties are involved, I'll have to refer you to the law book, because, frankly, I don't know. It's not a case of not remembering them offhand; I've just never had a need to commit them to memory. But, it's all in the law book, and the referee will make the call as she/he sees it anyway. And the referee is always right. Even when wrong. Which you can discuss over a beer or two *after* the game.

Drop kicks are another way of scoring points. Any time you have the ball in open field (and you're within range) you have the option of doing a drop kick for post. Spontaneously. Totally out of the blue. Surprise! Worth three points. The drop kick definitely has its roots in the old marauding mob village foot-ball games. Kicking for goal was always an option.

This sounds pretty simple. Well, if drop kicks were simple and easy, you'd see people drop kicking for post all over the place the whole game. The thing is that drop kicks were clearly invented primarily as a lesson in humility, and secondarily as a means of scoring points. You have to drop the ball – the ovoid, non-spherical ball – and then, *after* it has hit the ground, or just *as* it hits the ground, but *not before* it hits the ground, you have to kick it. I can whiff the ball, trying to do drop kicks on an empty field on a calm, sunny day with all the time in the world and no opposition. So, unless I'd suffered a sharp blow to the head, I would not be one to spontaneously do a drop kick for post in the middle of a game. Not everyone does drop kicks. Not many do them well. But, a few people do have a knack for it. I've probably witnessed no more than about a dozen in the ten years that I played.

One last scoring thing that I'll mention is the penalty try. If a player is about to score a try, and an opposing player does something illegal to prevent that player from scoring, the referee can award a penalty try (still worth five points). The penalty try basically says this: If the illegal play hadn't happened, the player with the ball would have almost certainly scored a try, and is thus deserving of the five points. It's in the spirit of the Advantage Law. To bring play back to where the penalty was committed would be an injustice to the team that, by all rights, should have scored. Penalty tries are generally not awarded in midfield. They're not all that common, either. But they're another part of the game.

There's still a lot about the mechanics of the game that I have not covered, such as exactly what the backs do when they run their plays (answer: run and pass), the kickoff (the team that just scored gets the ball kicked back to them, which is the opposite of football), the coin toss (captain's job), substitutions (allowed only to replace an injured player up until 1997, when the laws changed to allow up to five tactical or injury substitutions per match), timeouts (there are none, although a "minute" can be called to tend to or assess an injury), or the offside laws (the backs have to stay at least ten meters from the back of a lineout, and behind the last foot of the last player in a scrum, or ruck, or maul), or what happens when the ball goes out of bounds (lineout).

More on lineouts. The team that didn't touch the ball last before it went out of bounds gets to control the lineout. The forwards from both teams line up opposite each other, to form a tunnel, perpendicular to the sideline, starting five meters from the point where the ball went out. The hooker throws the ball in from the sideline, down the center of the tunnel formed between the two lines of forwards. It's a little like a jump ball in basketball, but with a lot more people. The team throwing in the ball has the advantage of knowing how deep the ball is going to be thrown, provided they can figure out their own calls. The basic idea, again, is that the forwards want to secure the ball and get it to their scrumhalf, who can then pass it out to the backs. And you know the rest. Well, enough of the rest.

Lineout between Beantown and Berkeley during the 2001 US Women's National Championship, played in Rockford, Illinois. (photo/rs)

chapter 7
the third half

Rugby is a very social sport, as evidenced by the age-old tradition of the rugby party. After the game, there is always a rugby party or "drink up," sometimes referred to as the "third half," which is hosted by the home team. It's like the rainbow after the thunderstorm, the keg of beer at the end of the pitch. Sometimes it's a veritable smorgasbord of good food and drink; other times it's bologna and white bread. The party may be held out at the field, at a rugby house, or at some bar willing to accommodate a bunch of muddy, sweaty rugby players.

I have always felt that it is a matter of rugby honor to put on a good party. This is probably left over from my U of I days when we may not have been able to beat the other teams on the field, but we could at least out-cook and out-cuisine them.

The drink up has its own traditions associated with it, including rugby songs and drinking games. And, maybe, some singing about drinking ("The first mate, he got drunk..."). There is a pretty wide range of rugby songs in existence. For example, back at Illinois, most of the songs we sang were simply borrowed from the men's teams and, let me tell you, they were crude. Sometimes the pronouns were changed, sometimes not, depending on personal preferences.

A friend of mine at the University of Illinois was studying sociology and sport, and actually wrote a master's thesis on the women's rugby subculture (Wheatley, 1987). In her thesis, she does a more detailed analysis of these songs from a sociological perspective. Imagine analyzing this:

My girlfriend's a bricklayer, a bricklayer, a bricklayer,
A very fine bricklayer is she!
All day she lays bricks, she lays bricks, she lays bricks,
And when she comes home she lays me!

The Beantown Song Book does not include the bricklayer song, and the songs tend to be more G to PG-rated. Some are traditional rugby songs ("Bread of Heaven," or "Cwm Rhondda," "The Wild Rover"), some are old favorites ("The Sloop John B," "Swing Low Sweet Chariot"), and some are take-offs on modern songs ("Bean Angel," sung to the tune of "Teen Angel," "California Beantown," sung to the tune of "California Dreaming"). And I must admit that the Amazons (Minneapolis) have historically done a pretty cute take-off on the theme to "The Brady Bunch."

Singing is a lot of fun, and is an integral part of the rugby culture. One night back in college, we had about half our team in one of the school's big red rental vehicles, which had come to be known as "travel pigs." (I don't really know how that started, but it's an apt description.) We were driving back to campus after a game in Missouri, when we just started singing every song that we could remember (and a few that we couldn't), and it was a blast. "Point Me in the Direction of Albuquerque," "Leavin' on a Jet Plane," "Country Roads." That genre. It made the trip go a lot faster. Of course, our trip home actually was faster – and shorter – than that of the other carload of players; they wound up driving back to Illinois from Missouri via Indiana. (Look at a map, and you'll see what I mean. You miss one exit in Effingham...)

The singing is probably one of the things I miss most about rugby, now that I'm retired. I remember a debate that I once had with an old college roommate: what was the greatest invention of humankind? I said it was the written word. Even as a college student, I was painfully aware of the fallibility and vagaries of one's memories, and figured that the invention of the written word must be the best thing, because then nothing would ever have to be forgotten. My roommate disagreed, and said that it was music, because you can say so much more with music than you can ever say with words alone.

Over the years, I have come to agree with her. Singing is primal; it likely pre-dates our species. (Is it really a human invention, then?) Outside of birthday parties, church, and the car, though, most people probably don't get the chance to sing very often. And yet, singing can be so exhilarating. Rejuvenating. This brings me to a line from *Don Quixote* (Miguel de Cervantes):

> Quién canta, sus males espanta.
> Translated: He who sings, scares all his troubles away.

It's taken out of context, but it's still true. It's a funny thing. I took voice lessons several years ago, because I wanted to learn how to sing with a little more confidence. I'd been playing my guitar, and had started writing a few songs here and there, but I was always shy about singing them out loud, so I thought this would help. I also thought it might just be fun, and maybe it would be another way to unwind and relax.

I went into these lessons thinking that I could go through my usual stressful day and then go to my music lesson and still sing with a nice, clear, open, relaxed voice, despite the fact that all the muscles in my neck and throat were still tight and tense as piano wires. What I learned is that it's all connected. Aaron Rae, my teacher, put it more eloquently: "Emotion is energy, and energy is neither created nor destroyed. It is simply transformed." So, all the stress, anger, and other pent up feelings from the day just came out in my voice during the lesson. It was kind of a vicious circle. I went into the lessons looking for peace, but learned that being peaceful was the prerequisite.

There's a song by Mary Chapin Carpenter, one of my favorites, called "It Don't Bring You." It's very peaceful, with an almost meditative cadence. It carries a similar message: you can't reap until you've sown. If you want kindness, then you must first be kind. If you want love, then you must first be loving.

So, voice lessons weren't the absolute answer to all my problems. I didn't stick with them, I just didn't have the discipline. But I did learn how to sing the scales both forward and backward. And I still play the guitar now and then, and I think it does leave me feeling better afterwards. (Other people also report feeling better when I stop playing…)

Singing can also set up a good sort of vicious circle. As in, the more you sing, the better you feel, and the better you feel, the better you sing. And so on. Opera singers reportedly have life expectancies some 20 years greater than the average person. A study by some Swedish researchers, reported in the British Medical Journal, supports this claim. Choral singers were found to have an 11 percent lower risk of dying over a nine-year period. And even people who regularly attended cultural events – such as theater, concerts, music, movies, museums, or sporting events – were found to have a 57 percent lower mortality risk compared to people who rarely attended such functions. Something about what we get from these events and activities affects our stamina for life. Upward spirals are as possible as downward spirals.

Speaking of downward spirals… Drinking is another way to scare one's troubles away, at least temporarily. It's also an important part of the rugby party. Unfortunately, it is probably not as healthful as singing, and sometimes only works to scare up new troubles.

There is a lot of drinking associated with rugby. No one is ever forced to drink. In fact, I know a couple of women rugby players who don't drink at all. But rugby would admittedly be a very difficult environment for a recovering alcoholic. If anything, rugby is probably very fertile ground for developing new alcoholics. It's an issue that is not often discussed. It's taken for granted that drinking and rugby go together. It's accepted. One team took an alternate view of the situation, and made up T-shirts saying: "My drinking team has a rugby problem!"

While the larger issue of latent alcoholism may go relatively unnoticed, I think most teams are at least cognizant of the drinking and driving issue, and encourage the use of designated drivers. If possible, tournament organizers try to hold the party at the same hotel where most of the players are staying. It's one thing to get wild and crazy, and then stumble up to your hotel room and throw up in the bag of team jerseys. It's quite another to get behind the wheel of a car.

In the first case, you'll only *wish* that you were dead when your teammates discover what a good time you had last night.

I am not lobbying to resume Prohibition. I enjoy a good nut brown ale, a dark heavy stout in winter, and nice, light lagers on sweltering summer days. Drinking can be fun, so long as it doesn't unnecessarily endanger innocent lives. That's all.

Because everything is a game in rugby, there are even drinking games at the party. One weekend, the Milwaukee women showed us a game that involved putting full cups of beer on our heads, and bobbing up and down, while singing, "Women of the sea go up and down like this…" I haven't seen this game in a while. As I recall, there wasn't a clear-cut winner, and it resulted in a lot of spilled beer, which I suspect may have dampened its popularity.

The most common drinking game across the board is the boat race, which has absolutely nothing to do with floating a craft of any sort on a body of water. About six players from each team line up across from each other, not so different from a lineout formation. They may pretend to be sitting like rowers in the hull of a boat. Everybody has a full beer. When the signal is given, the first boat racers from each team both start chugging their beers. The next person in line can't start chugging her beer until the rugger ahead of her has drained her cup, and turned it upside down on top of her head! The first team to finish wins. Of course, it is a matter of rugby honor not to spill any beer.

I was not a great chugger, and brought only shame and dishonor upon my team whenever I attempted to participate in a boat race, but I could make some pretty good brownies.

Poetic Interlude #2

Love life.
Live love.
Eat brownies.

Rosebud's Brownies

Preheat oven to 350º F.

Mix together dry ingredients:

2 cups sugar

1 cup flour

2/3 cup cocoa

1/2 teaspoon baking powder

1/2 teaspoon salt (or less)

Add wet ingredients:

3 eggs

2 teaspoons vanilla

3/4 cup vegetable oil & 1/4 cup water

To simplify measurement of oil and water, use a 1-cup measuring cup, and add water and oil to the top. You can vary the proportions of oil and water, just make sure the total is 1 cup. Mix together, and pour into a 9 x 13 pan. Bake for approximately 30 minutes, depending on your oven and personal preferences for moister or drier brownies.

Dashboard Treats

Forgot that you were supposed to bring a dessert to the party? You can make these during the game on a warm, sunny day.

Ingredients:

1 large can chow mein noodles

1 small bag chocolate chips

Open can of chow mein noodles, add chocolate chips. Replace cover and shake. Place can in warm location, such as the dashboard of a car.

Shake can occasionally (half time, between games) to redistribute melted chips. Allow to cool slightly before serving. Open can and serve. Remove can from dashboard prior to driving!

<u>Bread of Heaven</u>
(the song, not the recipe)

Guide me, Oh Thy great Jehovah,
Pilgrim through this barren land.
I am weak, but Thou art mighty,
Hold me with Thy powerful hand.

Bread of heaven, bread of heaven,
Feed me till I want no more,
Feed me till I want no more.

Open now the crystal fountain,
Whence the healing stream doth flow;
Let the fire and cloudy pillar
Lead me all my journey through.

Strong deliverer, strong deliverer,
Be Thou still my strength and shield,
Be Thou still my strength and shield.

When I tread the verge of Jordan,
Bid my anxious fears subside.
Death of death and hell's destruction,
Land me safe on Canaan's side.

Songs of praises, songs of praises,
I will ever give to Thee,
I will ever give to Thee.

This song, also sometimes known as "Guide Me, Oh Thou Great Redeemer," or "Cwm Rhondda" in Welsh, is a traditional church hymn, originally written by William Williams in 1745, and later translated to English by Peter Williams. Sometime later, after the creation of rugby, the song was adopted as a popular rugby standard, but it is most strongly identified with the Welsh national side.

chapter 8
rugby players play

Whether playing for a college club in the Midwest, or a city club on a coast, or anywhere in between, the women who play rugby all share one thing in common: their diversity. No, no, no. Just kidding. (That's supposed to be a joke.) Diversity will be covered later.

The common denominator I've observed is a certain intensity about living combined with an amazing capacity for play. Child-like, in fact. It's about eating the cream out of the Oreo first, and the cookie part last. Or, putting the cookie part back in the bag. Or in somebody's shoe.

I found something in my shoe one time. It resembled a dog turd. It turned out that one of my more creative (and mischievous) friends had saved the cookie she had gotten with the meal on the flight. It was a soft, chewy chocolate cookie, with a consistency similar to… Well, anyway, instead of eating her cookie, she decided to make a sculpture of it, and leave it for me to find in my shoe. ("Funny, smells like chocolate…")

Pranks are just another form of play. In college, we'd do animal calls. A bunch of us would get together and call people – usually teammates or players from other teams – and make all sorts of animal sounds when they answered the phone. Before we dialed the number, we'd each call off which animal we wanted to be. Now, thinking back on this, it all sounds kind of silly. Maybe it was a Midwestern thing. It's hard to explain, but it was a lot of fun at the time.

The pranks don't stop when you get out of school, either. The story goes that once upon a time, at a rugby tournament far, far away… Well, okay, it was in Georgia. But it was many years ago, when Beantown and Florida State University had a pretty strong rivalry. One of the Beantown players discovered FSU's bag of team jerseys left foolishly unattended out at the rugby fields. When her cohorts were alerted to this fact, they simply could not resist the temptation, and so STOLE FSU's entire bag of team jerseys. And then, to top it off, Beantown showed up at the party that night WEARING FSU's jerseys! You can just imagine the look on the Florida players' faces when Beantown walked in. They were in quite a state. And it wasn't Florida.

Rugby players like to play. And all this playing is done with a certain intensity. A few of the players I know are so intense, I imagine they even nap intensely. By "intense," I don't mean high strung, exactly, but highly focused. As in, "whatever you do, do your best."

Just because a body grows older and bigger, and has a job and maybe even a yard and a mortgage, doesn't mean that it has to forget how to be spontaneous and how to have fun. Sledding doesn't stop being fun once you cross a certain age threshold. It seems like, in our workaday world, we almost forget how to play. How many opportunities do we get to play each day? Are the opportunities there? Probably, but we just don't even see them anymore. It's hard to seize what you can't even see. And even if we do see these chances, we're often too busy and too tired to follow up on them. Play is not usually considered a necessity. It's not food, clothing, or shelter. But it is food, clothing, and shelter for the imagination. It's a chance for the mind and body to stretch and breathe and wander. It can be as revitalizing as sleep, and is probably just as necessary.

Poetic Interlude #3:

Sleep was like water
I drank it in
floated upon it
and let it carry me.
I just about drowned in it.
If you'd opened my door,
it would've just about
knocked you right over.

So we play. We dress up for Halloween. We go sledding and skating. We dance. We toss popcorn in the air and try to catch it in our mouths. We throw popcorn at each other. We play hide and go seek, Red Rover, Red Rover, amoeba tag, and mice-are-running-all-over. We put on skits, tell stories, go camping, and sing songs. It's like Girl Scouts for Grown-ups, but better. Because we're grown-ups, and we can do anything. And go anywhere. Or, more accurately, as my old college club used to say: "You can take us anywhere; you just can't take us back."

This brings me to the Rugby Road Trip, which is essentially an all-weekend-long traveling party with approximately 20 to 30 of your closest friends. Every weekend is a new adventure; you never know what's going to happen, but you can bet that it won't be boring. It may involve piling into someone's car to drive to Iowa, Michigan, or Philadelphia. And sometimes, it's about catching a flight to L.A., D.C., or Minneapolis. And, this is nothing compared to the Rugby Tour, which is like a two-week-long traveling slumber party in a foreign country. Traveling can be fun!

When you travel far, you usually wind up staying overnight. I've stayed in cheap hotels, with six or seven people to a room. And I've stayed in a few nice hotels, too. Often, if it's not a tournament, the home team will host the visitors. There's nothing like being picked up at the airport, being whisked away to someone's home, and being fed and taken care of. I have had the pleasure of staying with some wonderful rugby-hostesses.

Not every travel experience is so idyllic, though. Sometimes the flight is late. Sometimes you wind up sleeping on someone's couch or on the floor. And sometimes breakfast is a slice of toasted white bread, with old, yellowed margarine. And Kool-Aid to wash it down with. But, this would be the exception rather than the rule.

For better or worse, sometimes a rugby team is like having 20 or 30 younger and older sisters all at once. You really get to know your teammates, as well as the players on the other teams, during these trips. You're in close quarters the entire weekend. A lot of bonding happens in the process: the travel, the constant companionship, the goofing around, the party, and of course, ultimately, the game.

chapter 9
viva la différence!

The men and women who play rugby are very much alike in many, many ways: fun, playful, more than just a little wild, crazy, intense, passionate, and competitive. We all play the same sport, with the same laws, the same referees, the same ball, and the same fields. Rugby is rugby. The sport is modified in no way for women. The only difference is that women are on the field instead of men. Admittedly, the game looks a little different when women are playing. On average, men are stronger and faster, and so the men's game tends to move a bit faster, with more kicking. The women's game tends to focus more on finesse and discipline: passing the ball, and working plays. Similar to women's basketball in many respects.

And in other ways, the men and women who play rugby are very much *not* alike. Men's and women's rugby are at completely opposite ends of the spectrum when it comes to some aspects of the culture and attitudes surrounding the sport. Men's rugby has its own reputation and image issues to deal with. Some of the men's rugby teams have become legendary for their wild, drunken, raucous parties. It can be a sexist environment, though probably no worse than the NFL (cheerleaders, stupid commercials, etc.). To be fair, though, some men are very supportive of the women's teams. They love the sport, and believe women have just as much of a right to play. Some of these men are even married to women rugby players, leading to entire rugby families!

There may still be a few (very few) men who think that women should not be playing "their" sport. Over the past couple of decades, though, much progress has been made in reaching some common ground. The women's program has been earning the respect of the rugby community over the years by improving the overall level of play, and showing that the women are just as committed as the men to playing good rugby. It wasn't always that way, though. Let's take a look at how women's rugby got started.

chapter 10
a little herstory

The first recorded "ladies match" was played in 1913 in England, when Colonel Phillip Trevor's daughters and their friends insisted that they "simply must have a game" (*Rugby Union Football*). They convinced the good Colonel to referee the match, which he called "a very good first trial." Not much happened for many more years.

Although men started playing rugby in America around 1874, women didn't start playing here until the early 1970s. The first women's teams were formed in 1972 in Colorado, with the Rainbows (originally known as the Bumblebees) at the University of Colorado at Boulder, and the Hookers of Colorado State University. It has also been reported that another women's team was started at about the same time (and possibly even earlier) in Ridley Creek, North Carolina. Over the next several years, women's rugby teams started springing up on the east coast (Portland, Boston, Philadelphia, Cortland State, Williamsburg), in the Midwest (St. Louis, University of Illinois at Champaign-Urbana, Chicago), and on the west coast. The story I've heard in the Midwest is that the wives and girlfriends of the men's teams at the University of Illinois and St. Louis started talking, and decided that they too "simply must have a game." One of the first games in the Midwest was reportedly played between Saint Louis and the Mother Ruggers of Illinois in 1975. Many of these teams, including Beantown, Boston, Philadelphia and Chicago, have now been in existence for more than 25 years.

Of course there's much more to the story. Describing history is a little bit like being a sportscaster. I can either focus strictly on the dates and events, the play-by-play, or I can try to add some color, and put these events in some meaningful historical and cultural context.

First, it's important to understand just how different things used to be for girls and women in sports. Just how much the world has changed for girls and women even within the span of my own lifetime was brought home to me when I picked up an old book while browsing at a second-hand store: *The Girl's Book of Physical Fitness: An Excellent Guide for the Girl Who Enjoys Being Her Best*, by Jean C. Vermes (original Copyright 1961, but this was the completely rewritten and updated version, Copyright 1972), published by the National Board of Young Men's Christian Associations. The titles of other books penned by Ms. Vermes (with various co-authors) give a good indication of the times:

The Girl's Book of Personal Development
Pot is Rot
Helping Youth Avoid Four Great Dangers:
    Smoking/Drinking/VD/Narcotics Addiction
Male Power: The Young Man's Guide to Good Grooming

I don't mean to give Ms. Vermes a hard time. Frankly, many of the topics are still relevant, pressing public health issues today. The tone of the book is just a mix of Leave-it-to-Beaverish innocence and optimism overlain by shades of post-sixties awareness and modernism. This book was likely intended to inform as well as mold the beliefs of its young audience, similar to the old lined, scratched black and white 16 mm films they used to show us in grade school and high school, and now still frequently mocked on *The Simpsons*.

The Foreword, written by a doctor with the American Medical Association (AMA), notes that girls can and should participate in athletics, and reassures them that they can do so while maintaining their femininity. There was a great implied, underlying fear of a certain stereotype – the overly athletic woman. It's a good thing, even a healthy thing for girls to be physically fit. But, for goodness sake, you'd still better look and act like a girl.

Within the text itself, it is noted that there are still some exercises and sports that are unsuitable for girls (pole vaulting, weightlifting, and boxing), but that girls were starting to infiltrate historically male-dominated sports such as baseball, football, and ice hockey.

Infiltrate. I like that. It kind of makes us sound like spies. Since 1972, women have indeed succeeded at infiltrating even the unsuitable sports of weightlifting and pole vaulting. There are women who box, women who wrestle, and of course lots of women who play ice hockey now. I have the feeling that, if Ms. Vermes had heard of rugby at the time, she might have added it to her list of completely unsuitable sports. Or, maybe she would have wanted to play! Overall, I can't fault Ms. Vermes too much. I think she was trying to be as encouraging as she could be for the time. My point in bringing up this book is simply that these thoughts are not that old, and much has changed since 1972.

chapter 11
1972

The year 1972 would turn out to be a pivotal, landmark year for women in sports. It literally took an act of Congress, and the President's signature: Title IX (20 USC Section 1681). It was the dawn of a whole new era, when equal opportunities for girls and boys in school and sports became not just a good idea, but also the law. Whatever else he may have done, former President Richard Nixon deserves his due share of credit for his role in the passage of this legislation. Specifically, Title IX states:

> No person in the United States shall, on the basis of sex, be excluded from participation in, be denied the benefits of, or be subjected to discrimination under any educational program or activity receiving Federal financial assistance.

The final legislation was signed into law in 1975 by former President Gerald Ford, and included provisions that specifically prohibit discrimination in athletics. On the face of things, it seems like a matter of simple fairness: our daughters and sons should have equal opportunities in educational programs, both academic and athletic. Prior to Title IX, girls and women were caught literally in a no-woman's land. First, you have the AMA and others disapproving of girls competing with boys in contact sports. Of course, there would never be enough funding or interest for a school to create a separate girls' team. Can't play with the boys, and no girls' team to join.

Enter Title IX.

This legislation did not come out of nowhere, though. It came in response to what the people wanted. The National Organization for Women (NOW) had formed in 1966, and the women's liberation movement had developed a powerful voice. The nation as a whole had been worn down and torn apart by the Vietnam War, and was still dealing with a host of social issues left over from the 1960s: civil rights, drugs, the sexual revolution. Sex, drugs, and rock and roll. Authority was being questioned at every turn. People questioned their government, their leaders, and the war itself. There was the rise of a new form of investigative journalism, where the media acted as private detectives to bring the truth to the light of day, rather than simply the obedient mouthpieces of the government. Watergate was just around the corner.

In this climate, women also questioned everything they had ever been told about what women could and couldn't do, and their general station in life. The old answers no longer satisfied them, and so they started physically testing their own limits in every arena: school, work, athletics, politics, the military, the church, etc.

Women had been told historically that they could not run a marathon. This was proven wrong in 1966 when Roberta Gibb became the first woman to complete the Boston Marathon. She was not an official entrant because women were not allowed to run the Boston Marathon. The next year, Kathrine Switzer found a loophole, and managed to get an official entry number by simply signing her form, "K. Switzer." Pretty ingenious and devious of her. They naturally assumed that "K" was a man, and the officials were horrified when they realized that they'd been duped. The race director stopped her on the course, and tried to physically remove her from the race. Of course, her marathon effort became a rallying point for women who wanted more opportunities in sports. Finally – in 1972 – women were officially allowed to run the Boston Marathon, and on April 17th, Nina Kuscsik – not "N. Kuscsik" – won the women's division, with a time of 3 hours, 10 minutes, and 26 seconds. It would take another 12 years, though, before women would be allowed to run the marathon at the Olympics, with Joan Benoit Samuelson winning the gold for the US in 1984. All thanks to the renegade infiltrators of the 1960s.

Tennis was an accepted ladies' sport for many years, but the 1970s would see several challenges to the stereotypes of that time. In

1973, Billie Jean King would take on Bobby Riggs in the Battle of the Sexes – and win. That same year, a young sixteen year old tennis player from Czechoslovakia would make her entrance to the US women's tennis circuit: Martina Navratilova.

I was in grade school in the early 1970s, but I remember many of these things going on, sometimes only peripherally, in the background. But I definitely sensed that things were changing. I remember my best friend and I talking about becoming the first woman president and vice president someday. There was a sense that we could do anything, despite whatever obstacles might stand in our way, including just the simple fact that it hadn't been done before. It's strange to think about the way some things were set up then, and how biased they were. When I was in high school in the late 1970s, shop class was scheduled at the exact same time as girls' gym class, which was a requirement. It made it physically impossible for a girl to take shop. Social studies class was scheduled at the same time as home economics, assuming that only the boys would be interested in world affairs, and only girls would be interested in cooking and sewing. Freshman year, four of us girls took social studies. I had no interest in home economics then, but I was interested in the world. Sadly, it was assumed that someone couldn't be interested in both.

From a sociological standpoint, it's noteworthy that women turned to rugby in the 1970s, during what was likely a turning point for women in the United States. The early growth of men's rugby in the UK during the mid to late 1800s has often been interpreted as a response to the changing social trends of that time period. As women gained more power and freedom, men turned to rugby as a last male preserve, where they could display their masculinity and enjoy a no-girls-allowed boarding school camaraderie well into adulthood. Rugby was the proverbial clubhouse, where boys could still, always, just be boys. Reams have been written on the topic of the men's rugby subculture, and I would be remiss not to mention it. The interested reader can look to works by researchers such as Sheard and Dunning (1973 and 1979), and Donnelly and Young (1985), just to name a few.

A century or so later, women were no longer content to sit on the sidelines of this game, and so ventured forth into another heretofore boys-only terrain. It is somewhat ironic that men originally turned to rugby as an escape from empowered women, and then empowered women invaded the rugby domain in the 1970s.

chapter 12
1987

As the number of women's teams grew, tournaments were organized, and eventually regional select side (all-star) teams were formed. The first women's rugby national championship was held in 1978, with the team from Portland, Maine taking top honors. USA Rugby (the governing rugby body in the US) did not officially recognize the women's game at that time, so the first official national championship occurred the following year, and was won by Florida State University (FSU).

Many more years passed, more teams formed, and the first national select side team was formed in 1987. The team traveled to Victoria, British Columbia, and played its first test match (international) against the Canadian women, winning 22-3.

That's the play-by-play, but there was a lot more going on. If 1972 was a watershed for women's sports in general, 1987 would be the pivotal year for women's rugby.

The match against the Canadian select side was part of the Men's 12th Annual Can-Am Games, an event that was pretty well established by that point, and a fairly formal and prestigious affair. The men's teams were dealing with their own image problems, and there was an effort afoot by USA Rugby to try to get the men's rugby teams to be more responsible, do less damage to hotels, do less public vomiting and urinating, and so on and so forth, to be taken more seriously in the international rugby community.

The women were nowhere near as organized as the men's team at that time, and things were still fairly Bohemian. Just getting all the women's national team players to Victoria was an accomplishment, given that the women had to pay for their own travel, and had never played internationally before. There was some dissension at the time anyway between the men's and women's rugby communities, with the women wondering if they were getting their share of select side support from USA Rugby, and the men suspecting that the women were just draining the resources needlessly. For the most part, though, it was a live and let live atmosphere, until this tournament, when the Captain of the US men's team made the following remarks during an after-dinner speech at the post-tournament banquet:

> If women choose to play rugby, that's their right. But I don't and can't condone their bastardization of our great game. Men's rugby is a civilized war for survival and honor, and women can never play as men do. It's a travesty that my wife could travel two thousand miles to see this game and not be invited to this banquet – but these women could.
>
> *The Vancouver Sun*, November 16, 1987

As you can imagine, this turned into a small international public relations incident, as both women and men stormed out of the banquet hall. The fellow who made the speech eventually apologized for using the banquet as a forum for expressing his opinions, but he did not apologize for the way he felt.

One wonders if the whole nightmare could have been avoided if somebody had just given him a banquet ticket for his wife. I think it's okay though, and perhaps even necessary that this incident took place. The women had already recognized the need to improve the image of their game, but the Can-Am event galvanized the women's efforts to bring up the quality of their play to prove they took the sport as seriously as the men, and had just as much of a right to be on the field. This effort was already underway, as evidenced by the *Sports Illustrated* coverage of the 1987 women's national championship tournament held earlier that same year.

> The eight clubs competing last month at the ninth USA Rugby Football Union Women's National Club Championship brought a sober, solemn, almost dour approach to the game... 'We want to be taken seriously,'

said Candi Orsini, FSU's player-coach. 'Our emphasis used to be on the social aspect. Now we're concentrating on the beauty of the sport.' From an aesthetic standpoint, the fluid chaos of the final, between FSU and Boston's Beantown squad, could have been mistaken for a postmodern dance choreographed by Twyla Tharp.

Women ruggers are sensitive about their image. They already have a modest reputation as bruisers – you can hardly prance around looking like Billy Idol and expect to get a rep for daintiness. 'Male ruggers have to fight the image of hooliganism,' said Orsini. 'We have to contend with that as well as with the idea that we're more masculine than other women. It's frustrating."

Sports Illustrated, June 29, 1987

chapter 13
the talk

While the women's teams may have originated with the wives and girlfriends of the men's team, by the time I started playing rugby in 1986, the women's team at the University of Illinois had far fewer connections to the men's team. One of the men still helped coach on occasion, we still practiced on adjacent fields, and we still drank at the same dark, rugby and grad-student inhabited bar (Murphy's), but that was about it. It wasn't that the teams didn't like each other; they just didn't have that much in common.

This point may be best illustrated by explaining "the talk" that was given to the new players prior to the first game each season.

The first time I heard it was the spring of 1986, and we had been practicing for weeks, doing funny drills in the armory, doing more funny drills outside in the cold spring mud, and now we were about to have our first game of the season, traveling down to Southern Illinois University. Our captain called the team together after practice to have a talk. After all, the players on the team had a wide range of skills and experience, including quite a few rookies.

Our captain, who had been playing for about 17 seasons, spring and fall, from her Bachelor's Degree right through her Ph.D., was a very good player, but we all came to realize later that she was mostly a Master of Understatement. Every half-time or post-game talk would start with, "That was good, but..." We'd be losing to a bigger, better, faster team by a ridiculous margin, and still this is how she would start. I often wondered what exactly she had seen that was good.

That Thursday night after practice, it was declared time for our captain to give the "A-very-diverse-group-of-women-play-rugby" speech. So, we all gathered around to hear her speak.

"As you are probably aware, a lot of different types of women play rugby. English majors and engineering majors. Business majors and psychology majors. Freshmen, seniors, and graduate students. Tall women and short women. Fast and slow. And some women are straight, and some aren't. And it's not a big deal. But, if you have any questions, you can talk to any of us."

And so forewarned, off to Carbondale we went. And what did we see? Some very athletic women. Fun women. Wild women. Tired, aching, and bruised women. A few crew cuts. A few hairy legs. A few women kissing. Each other. Not during the game, obviously, but at the party afterwards. And that's okay, as Stuart Smalley would say. It really was very okay.

By the 1980s, women's rugby had developed a strong lesbian membership, as the sport provided a generally open and accepting environment for lesbian athletes. You could be strong, athletic, and play a truly physical, full-contact sport. Given the limited opportunities at the college level, rugby provided a venue for women who had played other sports in high school, or even no sport at all. Everyone came in having the same amount of knowledge about rugby: nada, zip, zero, nothing. We saw our first rugby ball at our first practice. We saw our first game first-hand, while we were playing in it. If that sounds a little crazy, well it was.

It was a wild and crazy time. The sport of rugby was founded on breaking the rules of the day, and in a similar vein, women's rugby in the 1980s was still a fringe element, decidedly a step off the beaten path. Not everybody was gay, and not everybody was straight, but for the most part, everybody was just very cool. Love and let love.

It was such a lesbian-centric atmosphere, though, at least one straight woman from that era reported that she was teased and harassed for being straight: "It's just a matter of time before we convert you." I don't think this was widespread.

The straight women who played, though, definitely had to have thick skins, and not worry about what other people thought of them. Rugby had a serious lesbian stereotype at this time. I feel bad that this type of harassment happened. On the other hand, it's an interesting turn of the tables, for someone who is straight to be

71

forced to justify or defend their heterosexuality. After all, couldn't it just be a phase?

At the start of the school year, various organizations would set up booths on the quad to attract new members. At the rugby table one year, we put up signs trying to describe the women who played rugby: Smart women play rugby. Athletic women play rugby. Strong women play rugby. Straight women play rugby. One passerby asked what that last sign was supposed to mean. (Duh!) We added another sign: Curvy women play rugby.

For whatever reasons, a lot of lesbians played rugby back then. It was no surprise, and was a completely accepted element of the landscape. Often times, the rugby party was even held at the local gay/lesbian bar, and the whole team – gay and straight – would be out on the dance floor together, drunk on battle joy and cheap beer, dancing to the synco-synthesized sound of the eighties – "You Spin Me Round (Like a Record)," "Boom, Boom, Boom (Let's Go Back To My Room)," "Bizarre Love Triangle," "It's Raining Men," and on and on the soundtrack goes. Those were the days.

There were many women who took their rugby quite seriously, but also seriously enjoyed the social aspect of the sport. It was some serious fun. Work hard, play hard. There were also some players who favored the party to the game, which realistically, probably made it more difficult for the sport to be taken seriously.

chapter 14
the rest of his story

So, this was the climate in which the 1987 Can-Am incident took place. Of course, I'd read about it at the time, and I've discussed it with various other players over the years, and generally the incident went down in the history books as the speech that sparked an outrage. How dare the captain of the men's team say that women should not play rugby?

Then, some early reviewers of the book commented that this same man had made monetary contributions to the women's national team in more recent years, an indication of progress. After all, my intention was not to dredge up any old ill will, but just to provide some perspective on the kind of thinking that was around not that long ago. Then, I got to thinking about it, and realized that I was basing everything on one newspaper article, and I wondered if there wasn't more to this story. Ultimately, I realized that I needed to get the proverbial rest of his story, and talk to him myself. There are always two sides (minimum!) to any story.

So I called Fred Paoli.

Yes, he said, the legacy of that speech has haunted him the rest of his rugby career. Perhaps it would be helpful to hear what had driven him to making those remarks in public.

When he saw his first women's game in the early eighties, somewhere in southern California, his immediate reaction was, "They're better than the men!" Fred had switched over to rugby from football, and recalled spending the first year just learning not to block people. The women of course didn't have all those hang-ups and bad habits inherited from football, and their game was much more fluid.

He had been around some of the women's teams at tournaments, and he was well aware of the whole lesbian element of the game, but it didn't matter to him. It was no big deal for a liberal Democrat like himself. But, these were local tournaments of little importance.

Victoria was a whole different ball game. The men's annual Can-Am games had been going on for over ten years. It was a fairly prestigious event. The day before the games, the Mayor invites both teams for a reception. After many years of nagging, the men showed up wearing coats and ties. After all, Fred had been dealing with improving the men's image problems for many years. The Canadian women wore nice skirts and jackets. And the US women showed up in jeans and T-shirts. I imagine they were very nice T-shirts and jeans. The women may counter that they had to spend all their fashion funds on traveling to Victoria. Maybe they weren't even aware of the tradition. In any case, this was strike one.

Next, during one of the games, Fred's in a lineout, and he looks over to the sideline, and what does he see? Two of the US women, in their jerseys, French kissing. There was a crowd of 5,000 at the games that day, including a very large youth rugby contingent. Strike two, Fred went from simmering to seething. Just for the record, it was pretty common to see two women kissing on the sidelines at women's rugby games in those days. It wasn't that unusual. That was the climate of things; there was very much of an in-your-face attitude. People just didn't care what others thought. It's possible that the kiss provided a hearty distraction for the youth, who had probably only read about such things. It may have taken some of the focus off the men's game on the field. In the women's defense, they were in Canada, where French is the native tongue. (This will not survive final editing, I am sure.)

Now, we get to the banquet. If Fred had any hopes that the US women had saved their fineries for the banquet, those hopes were shattered, as they arrived again in their preferred attire of jeans and T-shirts. And then, the US men and women got into a food fight. He wasn't sure who started it, but that was strike three, and he just boiled over. They were showing no respect for the tradition of the game.

Though, if you go back to the earliest foot-ball games of the early to middle part of the 2nd millennium, when the game consisted of marauding mobs chasing through the streets, this may have been a very appropriate, fitting tribute to the original tradition of the game.

Anyway, that's the rest of his story.

As a post-script to this first post-script, one of the women who was there provided some feedback. The women were not wearing jeans. Rather, they had been told to wear gray pants. Of course, none of their gray pants matched each other, and so, as she put it, they "looked like crap." I am no fashion guru (!), but even I can tell you that grays are very hard to match. There are so many shades of gray: charcoal gray, olive-gray, brownish grays, pinkish grays, warm grays, cool grays... They would have been so much better off to have gone with classic black pants instead. And, she thought the men started the food fight.

Again, my intention was not start a whole new round of debate, but strictly to put the development of women's rugby in some historical context. And history, as we know, can be quite complicated. Were the women wearing gray pants, jeans, or gray jeans? Were there women kissing on the sidelines? Who threw the first bread roll? And who really founded rugby? Was it William Webb Ellis or Jem Mackie? History is not black and white, it's gray. And there are many shades of gray...

chapter 15
the rest of herstory

After the events of 1987, the women's rugby program evolved and grew by leaps and bounds. Among the major developments, the Women's Rugby Football Union, which used to operate separately but parallel to the men's union, was absorbed into the USA Rugby Football Union (USARFU), now known as USA Rugby.

Around this same time, a more official distinction was made between women's college teams and city clubs. Historically, women's college teams and city clubs competed directly against each other. Often it was simply due to logistics. In the Midwest, for example, there weren't very many cities that had clubs (Chicago, Minneapolis, Milwaukee, Madison, and later, Columbus and Detroit). These teams were pretty much resigned to traveling great distances to play other city clubs. Even for the college teams, putting together a season, while keeping the amount of travel to a reasonable level, could be quite a challenge.

Many college teams also had a fair number of townies on the team, as there was nothing really prohibiting it, plus it was often difficult to field a full side in the early years. Willing players were never turned away. And a city club might have some college-age players who either weren't going to college, or went to a college that didn't have a rugby team.

Over the years, though, the number of city clubs grew, and the rules were changed to restrict the college teams rosters to primarily undergraduate students, with limited numbers of graduate students. At the same time, the city clubs were encouraged to play mostly other city clubs. The first separate Women's Collegiate National Championship was held in 1991, and won by the Air Force Academy.

The women's national select side also marked impressive achievements. The US Eagles took home the first Women's Rugby World Cup in 1991. The tourney was held in Wales, with teams from 12 nations participating. The US women won the cup with wins over New Zealand in the semi-final (7-0), and England in the final (19-6).

On their return, the US national team was invited to the White House. President George Bush wasn't available that day, and so the First Lady, Barbara Bush, hosted the ruggers, who all arrived in appropriate attire for the occasion.

The next World Championship Competition (which was technically not a World Cup due to a lack of official sanctioning by the International Rugby Board, or IRB) was held in Scotland in 1994. The US side crushed most of the competition in the early matches, but then fell to the English in the final (38-23). Alas, and no trip to visit the Clintons. Hillary would have understood; after all, it takes many villages to raise a rugby club.

It was clear that the English national program had made tremendous strides in just the 3 short years between 1991 and 1994. Meanwhile, there was an even greater rugby force brewing in the southern hemisphere: New Zealand. They didn't send a team to the 1994 competition (probably due to the sanctioning issue), but continued to invest a wealth of resources into their women's national side. This investment would pay off for them in the 1998 World Cup, played in Amsterdam, Holland. Again, the US team rolled through the early competition, to make it to the final, where they were decisively beaten by New Zealand, 46-12. The 2002 World Cup was played in Barcelona, Spain, where New Zealand swept the competition, defeating England in the final, and the US squad was relegated to 7th place.

The US Eagles – both the men and the women – face a number of challenges: they play and travel for their local club side, they come together to play as a team only a few times a year, and they need to work their day jobs to help support all of this travel. Other countries (such as New Zealand) have made it possible for most of its national side players to make rugby their day job. Simplifies things a lot. The US isn't at this point yet, so it may be a while before the next trip to the White House.

Another more recent development is the growth of the Under-23 select-side program (started in 1997), that gives young women the chance to compete internationally, and at a very high level, early in their rugby careers. Similarly, a National Women's Sevens team program was also started around 1995, providing another venue for international competition. Sevens is an abbreviated version of the game, with only 7 players on each side, and 7-minute halves. With fewer players, and just as much ground to cover, it's a game that generally favors the speed of the backs.

Based on 2003 statistics compiled by *Rugby Magazine*, there are currently 121 women's rugby clubs, and 319 women's college teams competing in the US. There are over twice as many teams as existed about ten years ago (61 club sides, 129 college teams in 1993). In addition, there are now 96 girls' youth teams. To put these numbers in perspective, there are a total of 1,905 rugby teams total in the US right now, and women's clubs represent about a quarter of that total number.

For more statistical details, and for monthly coverage of US rugby action, players should get themselves a subscription to *Rugby Magazine*. It also makes a nice gift for the rugger in your life. I'm retired, and I still subscribe. It's not just a report of statistics and tournament results, it's also a great source of information on the latest law changes, USA Rugby activities, training, nutrition, and more. It's the only consistent coverage of the game in the US (when's the last time your local newspaper ran a story on rugby?), and we owe them our support for the service they provide.

The women's collegiate division has been the fastest growing segment of rugby throughout most of the 1990s. The combination of school funding (available due to Title IX), and an increased popularity on college campuses has likely fueled this trend. The growth of college rugby has also trickled up to the club level, as many women are electing to continue their rugby careers after graduation. This pool of experienced players entering club rugby has helped generate a higher caliber of play across the board for the club sides. Consider that the first clubs often relied on players who had never even seen a rugby game before. The sooner women – and girls, and boys, and men – are exposed to rugby, and the sooner they play their first game, the closer we are to building our next World Cup teams.

Not only is college rugby good for rugby, though, it can be very beneficial for the players. There are all the things to be learned by playing team sports, that can't possibly be covered in a classroom or a textbook. Players take those lessons with them into their everyday life: Knowing when it's time to suck it up and keep pushing to reach one's goals, and knowing when it's time to take a minute. Knowing when it's time to stand one's ground, and knowing when to work towards a reasonable compromise. Knowing how to pull people together to strive for a common goal. And knowing when it's time to take a step back, and remember what it is that really matters.

I sometimes hear that college players don't see themselves playing once they have graduated. It's just a college thing. Rugby doesn't fit in with their perceptions of an adult lifestyle. They think they'll have to be dull, mature, and responsible. News flash: When you're a grown-up, you can still have fun, it's just that the limits of your playground have been expanded. Through some magic of mud, sweat, and sun, you will not age, so long as you play rugby. It is the mudbath of youth.

chapter 16
evolution and revolution

Women's rugby today is characterized by serious, fun-loving, committed athletes, who play simply for the love of the game. The culture has changed in some ways since the eighties, and has remained the same in others. The necessary infrastructure has been established for the sport to be more competitive, and thus taken more seriously. Various select-side teams and venues have been developed to groom future World Cup players, and the college program is a well-organized structure of its own. College teams and club sides play in separate divisions, although it's not unusual for a college team to occasionally play a club's B-side just for the challenge and experience.

Culturally, you're less likely to see two women kissing on the sideline, and it's less likely (but not impossible) that the party will be held at the local gay/lesbian bar. Rugby is no longer a huge lesbian social networking vehicle. On the other hand, I've heard that there are still teams that give some version of "The Talk" before the first game weekend, or playing a club side. Lesbians are still an accepted part of the rugby landscape. Wherever one goes and plays rugby, it will come as no surprise to anyone that there are lesbians in their midst. This acceptance is a holdover from the eighties, retained as a part of the sport's rich cultural history. It's a non-issue for the most part. It just doesn't matter.

But it matters that it doesn't matter, and let me explain why. To play the devil's advocate, why should it matter what people do in their spare time? All that should matter really is what the players do once they take the field. Race, religion, relationships, all that stuff, shouldn't matter. The only thing that should matter is the level of performance on the field.

The reality, though, is that we take with us our whole selves to wherever we go and whatever we do, whether it's work or play. It's difficult to dissect and separate the different hemispheres of a person's life. Sit next to a guy at work who has had a new baby, and there is no way (unless he's an android) that you won't hear about the new baby. You will know when the baby starts sleeping through the night, starts teething, or runs a fever. I'm not complaining, but I think it's important for everyone to recognize that as humans, we are all multi-dimensional beings.

For many women, the rugby community may be the most accepting and affirming environment they have, where couples' relationships are both acknowledged and affirmed. Those two women aren't just roommates, and we respect that. Lesbians may not get this much support from their family, church, or workplace. Consider the range of what you might experience at work, anything from outright discrimination on the basis of sexual orientation, denial ("don't ask, don't tell"), or acceptance, such as extending benefits to include domestic partners. (It is amazing that a saying my cousin Joe and I threw around in our adolescence – "ask me no questions, and I'll tell you no lies" – could be turned into official policy by the government.) For all these reasons, it is noteworthy and meaningful that the rugby environment recognizes and affirms lesbian relationships.

While the rugby culture has evolved to be more serious over the years, with less emphasis on the lesbian element, the culture of American society has also evolved over the past several decades to become more tolerant and accepting of gays and lesbians. As society becomes more accepting, it becomes less necessary for gays and lesbians to be a fringe element, and have an in-your-face attitude. At some point, the mainstream and the fringe meet somewhere in the middle. As the mainstream has become more accepting of homosexuality, lesbians and gays have become more like the girls and boys next door. Which happened first, the chicken or the egg? The acceptance or the acceptability?

Evolution and revolution both imply change, the only difference is the speed at which the change takes place. Small, furry rodents evolved into humans (we think) over a period of millions of years. That process was evolutionary. If you could build a machine that could turn a mouse into a human overnight, that would be revolutionary. Revolutionary changes have occurred in American society over the past several decades, as a result of the slow evolution of beliefs and suppositions. Paradigms have shifted.

The gay rights movement had its start in 1969 with the Stonewall Inn rebellion in New York City's Greenwich Village. Police raids were as routine as they were brutal and demeaning. Everyone has a breaking point, and in the early morning hours of June 28th, the patrons of the Inn reached theirs. Why not – what did they have to lose? They'd just bid a final farewell to icon Judy Garland hours earlier; she had always promised a place somewhere for them, over the rainbow, and now she was gone, too. Drinking and drugs also may have played a part in fueling the rebellious spirit. It was just unheard of, unthinkable, that these people would rebel. The dominant thought at the time was that they would go quietly, as they always had, out of shame, and fear of being recognized.

Not caring what other people think is a very liberating force. Suddenly, a faceless underworld that existed only in the shadows was brought into the light and very real, human faces were revealed. This was the start. It was possible to be both gay and proud.

The AIDS crisis, first recognized in the early 1980s, also forced the gay community to become more visible. For many, it was a decision, to either die in silence or speak out. One of the mottos of this era was "Silence = Death." If you're going to die either way, do not go gently – or quietly – to this goodnight. Many high-profile men with AIDS came out, whether they wanted to or not, either when they became sick, or after they'd passed on. It is pure tragedy, the human loss from this disease. It was not a faceless tragedy, though. A lot of people were discovering that a gay man could look a lot like their son, brother, cousin, or uncle. And they didn't love them any less.

One of the greatest forces of change has been giving a face to the gay and lesbian movement. Think back to 1987 – who was out? Who could America look to, and say "this is a gay man or woman." I am wracking my brain, and all I can come up with is Martina

Navratilova (if people read her 1985 autobiography), Harvey Milk, and we suspected Elton John and Boy George, though there hadn't been any official pronouncement yet. My old *Webster's New World Dictionary* from around 1980 (which I still have and use occasionally) doesn't even have dyke as an entry; it just goes right from dying to dynamic. Some of its newest entries, as advertised on the back cover, included ethnicity, granola, hatchback, and Watergate, which should give you a little sense of the times.

Where were other gays and lesbians? In music, k d lang and the Village People were within the popular realm. Even then, the Village People were not categorized necessarily as being a gay group; they were just guys who were very enthusiastic about staying at the YMCA and being in the Navy. If people really thought about it, they might have suspected as much, but it certainly wasn't a topic suitable for dinner conversation.

There was an entire subculture of lesbian music, as evidenced by the Michigan Womyn's Music Festival. There were some wonderful musicians who never attained fame with the popular masses, but fed an appreciative audience hungry for their music – Chris Williamson, Ferron, and all the rest. But, these acts were not on the radar of mainstream America.

Were there gays and lesbians in the movies pre-1987? The only lesbian movies I can think of are *Desert Hearts*, and *Personal Best*. Oh, and Cher played a lesbian in *Silkwood*.

There have been three marches on Washington, DC, for gay and lesbian rights (1979, 1987, and 1993), with attendance ranging between 100,000 (1979) and 800,000 (1993). The posters supporting the marches give a telling picture of the mood at each march. The 1987 march was characterized by the poster, "Come out, come out, wherever you are!" This strategy recognized the power of giving a human face to the movement, to show what gays and lesbians looked like: everyday people. A poster from the 1993 march was a little more aggressive, even confrontational: "We're here, we're queer, get used to it!"

A lot of people followed the advice of the 1987 poster and did come out. A lot of men were forced to come out, by recognizing that they had AIDS. A good number of everyday people also came out, risking the loss of their jobs, the loss of family support, and potential community retribution. Sometimes, the results were tragic. And sometimes it was anticlimactic. As a friend's dad put it, "Twenty years you've been coming home with nothing but girls. What, do you think I am, stupid?"

If everyday people could come out, why shouldn't the celebrities, who were in a much more financially secure position? Of course, that position balanced delicately on their continued popularity with the masses. Who has come out since 1987? The following list is by no means all encompassing, but it should give you a sense of the numbers involved. A Democrat in the White House probably helped the movement, too. I'm not sure this list would be as long otherwise. Here goes: Melissa Etheridge (yes she is), Ellen Degeneres, Chastity Bono, Barney Frank, and Rosie O'Donnell, just to name a few.

What about TV and movies? Since 1987, we've seen popular movies with lesbian themes and main characters: *Go Fish*, *The Incredible True Adventures of 2 Girls in Love*, *When Night is Falling*, and *Bar Girls*. On television, we've watched "the kiss" break new ground on L.A. Law, Ellen's sitcom (*Ellen*) venture into uncharted territory, *Will and Grace* (of course), and even Erica Kane's daughter, Bianca, deal with coming out on daytime soap institution, *All My Children*.

The resounding message: We are everywhere. And nobody cares that much anymore. But it does matter, because for so many years it mattered all too much.

chapter 17
femininity defined

After all that has been said so far, someone somewhere is probably thinking, "well, gay or straight, these rugby players don't sound very feminine." Soapbox, please.

First, let's look at what it means, to be feminine. If you check out the dictionary definitions, you'll find words like gentle and delicate. It makes us sound like fine washables, silk, wool, and rayon. Hand wash only, and block flat to dry. That's the message that has been overtly and subliminally communicated to girls and women over the years. Of course, women have been tough, as tough as they've needed to be, as tough as the times required. Women bear children after all. But the message was that women, as the weaker sex, required greater protection and special treatment.

The problem with making such generalizations, though, is the inherent problem found anytime when using averages to represent a population. Averages don't do a good job of accounting for the variability within a population. Statistically, the average misses the far ends of the curve. And, that's if a population even conforms to a neat statistical formula!

Perhaps the word feminine needs to be defined more expansively, to fit the population it is describing. Feminine is as feminine does, as Forrest Gump might say.

"What it is to be a woman" covers a large amount of territory. There is tremendous variability among individuals. Even one woman may have any number of changing roles and experiences through the course of her lifetime. And a woman may change how she interacts and presents herself through the course of a single day, depending on the situations.

How does femininity fit into this? What is it? Will we simply know it when we see it? It must be tied into the averaging business somehow, because it's considered the "norm" for females, to be feminine. Femininity has been a stereotype, a caricature, an average. And the more you resembled that ideal, the more feminine you were, and that was generally taken as a good thing. It was a yardstick to be measured up against – or to fall short of. And yet, the individuals at the far ends of the curve – aren't they still women? Or, as Sojourner Truth said, "Ain't I a woman?" She was responding to a heckler who had proclaimed women unworthy of the vote because of their status as the weaker sex. Her famous speech from the 1851 Woman's Rights Convention, held in Akron, Ohio, follows.

> That man over there says that women need to be helped into carriages, and lifted over ditches, and to have the best place everywhere. Nobody ever helps me into carriages, or over mud puddles, or gives me any best place! And ain't I a woman? Look at me! I have plowed and planted, and gathered into barns, and no man could head me! Ain't I a woman? I have borne 13 children, and seen almost all of them sold off into slavery, and when I cried out with my mother's grief, no one but Jesus heard me. And ain't I a woman?

This entire discussion may seem irrelevant; it's just an adjective. So what if some women are more – or less – feminine than others?

Much of the feminist movement of the 1960s and 1970s dealt with how women were perceived in society, and how women perceived themselves. Over the years, femininity has been used as justification both for protecting women, as well as for restricting women. Because you are weaker and gentle and delicate, you must be protected from the harsh, cruel world. And therefore, you also could not possibly be capable of doing these other things. The limits of what women should and could do were defined by a male-dominated society, and instilled in women from the time they were little girls.

Imagine as a child, being told that you shouldn't go running, lift weights, or otherwise strain yourself. Imagine as a child being told that there was no need for you to finish high school, or to go to college. It wasn't that long ago.

These myths were passed down, from generation to generation, and were considered cultural fact. And if they were questioned? "Because that's the way it has always been." What change has come, has not come quickly or easily. All the expectations and trappings associated with what is considered feminine have been deeply ingrained both in society at large, and within the minds of women. These expectations can become a self-fulfilling prophecy. Many a woman along the way has had to stop and ask herself: Whom do I believe? Those who say what I can and can't do, just because I am a woman? Or my own mind and body? All the soul searching and consciousness-raising of the 1960s and 1970s laid the groundwork for the many advances of the women's movement.

What is consciousness-raising anyway, but stopping and stepping back to take an objective look at our beliefs system, disentangling ourselves from our cultural inheritance, and examining the basis for those beliefs and values.

This whole discussion probably seems like very ancient history today. All these battles have been fought and won, and they're done. Yes, of course, women can vote, go to college, enter any career, have their own credit history, get a loan, and buy property. What more could you want?

With comfort comes complacency. Is there even a need for a feminist movement today? Some people would say we have come as far as we need to go. A lot of women don't see the need to get all worked up over "women's issues." In fact, it's probably accurate to say that it has become unstylish to call oneself a "feminist," or even be a member of NOW. Nobody wants to burn their bras anymore. Hey, we need those sports bras to go running, and to go to aerobics class! It has taken years for good sports bras to become available. They did not even really exist in the 1970s, and good ones were still hard to find in the eighties. And I'm not trying to burn anyone's bra! But, I feel like we have become complacent. Things are pretty good for women. Why make waves? Young, cool, hip women don't want to be associated with organizations that are stereotyped as a bunch of middle-aged, extreme, radical, political feminists. They have been empowered, and they feel in control of their destiny. The mundane, everyday issues of the glass ceiling, family policy issues (maternity leave, family sick leave, access to affordable child care, etc.), and discrimination and harassment in the workplace seem to be other people's problems.

Even though society has undergone vast change, we're still not there yet, on two counts. First, there are continued attempts to reverse the forward steps taken over the past several decades. Title IX has been subject to repeated attacks over the years, primarily by those wanting to protect or increase football budgets. It's about power, equal opportunities, and a misplaced sense of entitlement. Does a level playing field put men at risk? Not necessarily. Only if one believes that women's gains translate into men's losses.

This is the second count: We were sold a bum bill of goods in the early days of the feminist movement. We were told that we could have it all. Career and children, no problem. The traditional roles of women – mother, housewife, teacher – were generally undervalued by society at that time. "She doesn't work, she's just a housewife." (Just raising the next generation of humankind.) It seems like the early feminists wanted to distance themselves from these traditionally female roles, and open the doors to careers that were valued more highly in society, and were typically held by men. Indirectly, and probably unintentionally, there was almost some sort of fem-phobic denial of the biological reality that women give birth to babies, and are responsible in large part for their care.

Today, it is the exception for a parent to stay home with the children. Often, economic realities force both parents to work, given the ever-increasing costs of housing and higher education. There are a number of pros and cons to this situation. The benefits: women feel more empowered, feel less dependent on their partner, and get to enjoy the mental and social stimulation of working outside the home. The downside: the difficulty in finding quality, affordable daycare for the children, and juggling work with everything else that our culture says women should be doing (shopping, caring for elderly relatives, planning holidays, etc.).

Decades ago, the feminist movement distanced itself from child rearing. It was menial, low-paid work that could be done by anyone. Tell this to someone now trying to select a daycare provider. They do not want just anyone caring for their children! In fact, they would prefer someone who is first-aid and CPR-trained, trilingual, Mensa-registered, and has a master's degree in child psychology. The reality is that no matter whom the parents pick to watch their children, it is difficult for them to trust a stranger with their offspring.

Politicians bandy about the term "family values" as though it's a packaged set to which all good, traditional families subscribe. Kind of like the *Encyclopedia Britannica* or *Good Housekeeping*. More often, it seems like a code word that gives some people permission to hate and discriminate against other people. It gives them a platform, a basis from which to attack. Wouldn't we all be better off, though, if less was said about family values, and more was done about simply *valuing families* in whatever shape, size, or form they take?

Ironically, our society looks at daycare as the parents' problem – hey, you were the ones who decided to have children, now deal with it. A simple answer to a complex problem. Question: How important are children to the future of our society, and humankind in general? Answer: Kids *are* the future society. And so, society as a whole needs to take an interest in these children. We have a vested stake in how they are being cared for and educated. This vested interest just needs to be converted into programs and policies: longer paid maternity leave, flexible work place, flexible work hours, and more quality, affordable daycare. These ideas are not just good for the parents and the children, but they benefit all of society. We must all shoulder the burdens of raising the next generation.

It may sound like I'm advocating a giant step backwards, but I'm not. The most important thing that has come out of the feminist movement is the freedom for women to choose the path that is right for them. It is okay for women to make any choice: to have a career, to have children, to have both. To play rugby. Not every woman is going to do everything. But, if a woman wants, she should be able to pursue the calling of her choice. The element that is missing is the support in society and in the work place to facilitate making these choices. There is still much to be done, but I will step down from my soapbox now.

chapter 18
politics and violence

We've already talked about one possible reaction to women's rugby that could be expected from the general populace ("that doesn't sound very feminine"). How would crunchy, radical, political feminists view it? I've heard two reactions. Some get pretty excited: "That just makes such a wonderful, political statement about the power of women." Some get worried: "That sounds very violent." Well, one issue at a time.

As far as making a political statement, I think you first have to decide whether or not the women's intentions matter. Do the women have to be intending to make a social/political statement by playing rugby, in order to make such a statement? A very wide variety of women play rugby, with views ranging from highly political to apolitical to anti-political. The vast majority of women play rugby simply to play rugby. I mean, if you want to make political statements, there are a million easier ways of doing so, without going to practice sessions several nights a week, and coming home aching and bruised after the games every weekend. I think most of the women who play, though, do appreciate the fact that playing such a physical sport certainly makes a statement about the capability of women to be strong and aggressive. Whether intended or not.

Next question: Are women also capable of violence? First, we need to distinguish between the physical nature of the game, and individual behaviors that cross the line. It's a very passionate sport. It's easy for tempers to flare. If somebody takes a swing at another player, I'd have to call that an act of violence. And there is now a penalty system in place enabling the referee to remove a player for this type of behavior. They may be sent off, to the "sin bin," for a period of time, and may be subject to additional suspensions.

If someone makes a good, hard, clean tackle, they were just doing their job. They didn't do anything that the other player wasn't expecting. "I have the ball, and you want it. Of course you're going to try to tackle me." It's just like chess, when one player says checkmate, and then takes the other person's king. Except that rugby is played using our bodies, instead of little castles, bishops, and horses and things. And rugby is played on a patch of earth roughly 70 meters wide by 100 meters long, not on a 12-inch by 12-inch board. But, otherwise, rugby and chess are alike, in that they are both about strategy. The strategies are simply executed in very different fashions.

chapter 19
what about injuries?

The question comes up, "What about injuries?" Well, I'm not going to lie. It's a physical sport, and even if not intentionally violent, injuries can and do happen. Mostly minor (scrapes, bruises, and pulled muscles), but some are more serious (concussions, broken bones, and various joint injuries). And, there are the rare, but real occasions where people have become permanently disabled, or have even died from rugby injuries. You could lose the ability to walk. Or talk. Or even breathe. The head, neck, and spine are particularly prone. In spite of all the conditioning and training, all it takes is being in the wrong place at the wrong time. One freak hit. It is possible to die playing rugby; it's also possible to die crossing the street. There are a million senseless ways to die, and perhaps rugby is just another one of them. The sheer act of living can be dangerous; and rugby is perhaps living dangerously, always aware of the bullet that has just been dodged.

What happens when a player gets hurt? The player can request an injury minute, and the referee will typically stop the game and award the minute at the next convenient stopping point. The flow of the game is key. In that minute, the player can have the injury tended to, catch a breath, and perhaps shake it off. It's quite common to see someone take a minute, get something taped up, and go back into the game. If the injury is more serious, then a decision has to be made about whether or not the player should come out of the game. I've seen a player come off the field with a broken collarbone, getting ready to go to the hospital, asking her teammates how many weeks it would take to mend, and how long it would be before she could play again.

Bones mend. Cuts and scrapes heal. Bruises eventually go away. Other injuries, however, can spell the end of a rugby career, such as certain knee and back injuries. And many of us are pretty much resigned to a high probability of having arthritis as we get older. Not everyone can play rugby. If you already have bad knees, or a bad back, this is probably not the sport for you. And those who do play realize they won't be able to play forever.

There are certainly risks involved in playing rugby. Everyone who plays is aware of it. For this reason, rugby players take their training and conditioning very seriously. Being in good shape and stretching properly can significantly reduce the chances of injury.

People get injured playing all kinds of sports. The weekend athlete who picks up a game of softball or basketball without stretching properly, also risks injury. I'm not going to do a comparative risk analysis, or anything like that. Sure, you can get hurt doing just about anything, anywhere. In rugby, though, the risks are laid out on the table at the start. The players do what they can to be in the best physical shape possible to play, and learn proper playing techniques (especially in the scrum) to minimize their risk of injury.

Sports such as soccer, softball, and basketball are technically considered non-contact, but the reality is that contact happens. Rugby, on the other hand, makes no bones about it (so to speak). There will be contact. There's an old saying about rugby and soccer that goes something like this:

Soccer is a sport made for gentlemen, played by hooligans.
Rugby is a sport made for hooligans, played by gentlemen.

Because contact is inherent to the sport of rugby, a certain sense of decorum about the contact exists. You don't need to sneak in an illegal hit when the referee isn't looking. There are ample opportunities to make perfectly legal contact with your opponent, all while playing within the laws. There is not a great incentive to sneak illegal contact into a rugby game for a number of reasons. First of all, it will probably just annoy the other team; the next time they see your jersey number, they'll remember what you did to one of their own, and likely return the favor. Secondly, it does nothing for the development of your game. You won't always be able to get away with it. The ref may not have seen it today, but the ref next weekend may penalize you for it. Who wants to develop a game plan designed around cheap shots? The goal is to play good rugby.

chapter 20
why?

I think by now we've covered enough of the *how* rugby is played, and even some pretty good reasons why people would *not* want to play rugby.

A perfectly valid question is *why*? Why do people play this crazy sport? Simply put, it's as fun as it is intense, and it is this combination that makes it such a unique and satisfying experience.

The physicality of the sport is part of what makes rugby so intense. First of all, you may recall that in the description of the kit, the topic of padding was mentioned nowhere. That's because in the bad old days, when I started playing rugby, there really wasn't much in the way of padding used; the laws didn't allow it. I remember literally taping big mittens to a friend's ribcage one time, because she'd hurt her ribs. You could use protective wraps to keep an injured part from harm, but they could not have any hard or sharp parts. Mittens fit the bill in that case. Players wore what suited them and their position. Some hookers wore shin guards. Almost all the second rows wore a scrumcap or at least tape (athletic or electrical) around their heads, to keep their ears from getting chafed and scraped too badly. A few players wore kneepads; I was afraid they'd slow me down. And practically everyone wore mouth guards. More than once has a new mouth guard been formed in a cup of hot water at a local restaurant on the way to the game.

That was then, and this is now.

The International Rugby Board legalized the use of soft foam torso pads and headgear around 1997, and it seems like more and more players are giving them a try. When these pads first came out, they created a bit of controversy. It is undeniable that being able to crash into someone, and have much of the impact absorbed by the padding, gives a player an advantage, both physically and psychologically.

One of the basic tenets of the game always seemed to be that the force of impacts would be limited by the human element of the game: how fast players run, how much they weigh, etc. And it goes both ways. As hard as you collide with someone, you're both going to feel it, which seems fair. You're not going to deliver a blow that you couldn't take yourself. Which is why people felt the new pads gave the few players who wore them an unfair advantage.

Part of me would like to say, "Hey, we didn't have all these pads around when I started playing. We had mittens, that's what we had! And we didn't allow all these substitutions, either. If you were selected for a match, you were in the game for the duration. You played until you couldn't. Then, and only then, would we let you come off the field." Ah, yes, the good old days. It was just a few decades ago when almost no one wore seat belts, and we were constantly barraged by commercials extolling the virtues of smoking, and how cigarettes would make us more attractive. Things change; sometimes even for the better.

Even with the new padding, rugby is still not American football. There are no huge, hulking shoulder pads, and no helmets hiding people's faces. You know your opponent in rugby as another flesh and blood human being, and not some faceless entity. You may have even slept on their couch the night before.

In rugby, there is very little separating you from your opponents, the ground, or the elements. You are literally a part of the game. It's not like tennis where you use a racquet to hit a ball back and forth. It's more like playing tug of war with the tennis ball. It's hands on. And it's not a neat, tidy paved rectangle. You're out in the elements.

I have never seen a game cancelled due to weather; the only acceptable reason for suspending play is thunderstorms, due to the risk of lightning. Otherwise, I've played in snow squalls and downpours, in the cold and in the heat, on fields that were more mud than grass, and on dusty, hard dried-out surfaces, with rocks and sticks, plus the occasional bottle or can, or other nasty piece of refuse. And there have been the games played on lush, soft, bright green grass. Artificial turf is no good for rugby; rugby is about being real.

Our modern culture tends to isolate us from the natural, physical environments. Our surroundings are filled with too much plastic, glass and steel. The real world is messy in comparison. Even personal contact is minimized, it seems. You bump elbows with someone at the coffee maker at work, and it's "Oops!" and "Sorry, excuse me!" We avoid eye contact with strangers in cars, on buses, and at the supermarket. It is easier not to acknowledge another human's existence.

To carry this to the extreme, look at modern warfare. It has come a long way from the days of bayonets and seeing the whites of the enemies' eyes. Instead, we try to do our business with air power, smart bombs and surgical strikes. All with the press of a button, making it seem all the more like a giant video game. I understand that the air approach saves the lives of our ground soldiers, but it makes it more difficult to comprehend the reality of what's taking place. There is little need to think about the pain and suffering of the real people at the receiving end of our weaponry. We are so far distanced from it all, we risk losing our capacity for empathy.

Rugby is a different world from all of this. It's a physical sport, where it's a given that you're going to come in close contact with other people. In fact, you often wind up intimately entangled with other players. It's like a giant Twister game that has gone awry. You are also directly in touch with the elements. Whatever it's doing outside, you're out there in it. In a way, you're very exposed, even vulnerable, when you play rugby. Not in a bad way. Just a very real way. Rugby has also been described as a very sense-ual sport, which seems fitting, as you're experiencing the game on many levels and through all of your senses.

Even the way that contact is made in rugby differs markedly from most other sports. There is no blocking, as there is in football. It's not allowed. Whoever has the ball is fair game. Besides, anyone who might be in such a position, downfield of the person with the ball, would be offside (useless). The only way you can support the player with the ball is to be in a position to take a pass from them, or to bind onto them and help drive if a ruck or maul forms. The game is not geared toward protecting the one with the ball and the golden arm. (Although it is preferable for the forwards to get the ball out cleanly to the scrumhalf.) Everyone takes hits. It's about being there in support of your teammates when they take the hit.

Rugby is a very demanding sport, both physically and mentally. Games typically consist of two 40-minute halves, with a 5-minute halftime break. In other play, at the collegiate level, and in tournaments, the halves may be shortened to 30 minutes each. Except for injuries, there are no timeouts and limited substitutions. Play is continuous.

There's also a version of rugby called "sevens," that's most often played in the summer. It's called sevens not only because there are seven players on each team, but also because the halves are only seven minutes long each. I've been teased by co-workers for driving hours to play minutes worth of rugby. But, with less than half the usual number of players to cover the field, seven-minute halves are quite long enough, especially on a muggy Midwestern summer day. The game of sevens is a great test of sprint-endurance. I usually just tell myself that I can do anything for seven minutes. And if I can make it through seven minutes, I can make it through fourteen minutes. (I once used this sort of rationalization to convince myself that I could run a half-marathon. "Since I jogged three miles two weeks ago...") There's an old Zimbabwe proverb that comes to mind:

> If you can walk, you can dance.
> If you can talk, you can sing.

Although mostly a game for backs, sevens is played by forwards, too. For example, there is a sevens team called the Turbo Props, made up entirely of props from various teams. Their motto is: If we catch ya', we'll kill ya'. Don't worry. They're just kidding. I think.

Continuous play means that everyone has to be heads up all the time, for every play, for all 14, 60, or 80 minutes. To get where you need to be, at any given moment, you must be in great physical shape, in terms of endurance, strength, speed, and flexibility. I've heard it said that the average forward typically runs about six miles in a game. It's not a sport to be taken lightly. One doesn't "sort of" play rugby. Rugby requires too great of a commitment for that. No time-outs. No free substitutions. No spacing out. You have to be physically and mentally present for the duration.

There's that term used in sports called sucking it up. I have no idea where it came from. It has probably always been around. George Washington may have even used the term at Valley Forge. It's about not letting the fact that you're down, exhausted, or hurt, get in the way of getting to the next play. It's when your legs are shaking and feel like they're made of wood, and your lungs are burning and feel like they're about to explode. That's when you suck it up, and you get yourself where you need to be for the next play, or make that next tackle, or run with the ball with all you've got. This is the visceral part of the game, when you're running on pure emotion and adrenaline. When you feel like you have nothing left at all to give, you look somewhere deep inside yourself, and somehow find more. You discover that you are stronger than you know. It's always a revelation.

It's not often in our everyday world that we are tested to our limits in such a fashion. Except for boot camp, war, and Ph.D. theses, perhaps. Think about it. When was the last time you ran as fast as you could, pushed as hard as you could, or threw yourself into something with all you had? It's a great feeling. What really adds to this is the sense of team-ness. When fifteen players pull together on the field, working to be there for each other, you have something far more powerful than fifteen individuals. Everyone who has ever played a team sport knows this sensation. The technical term for it is synergy. It's when karma gains momentum. It's the nonmathematical equation that says: $(1+1+1+1+1+1+1+1+1+1+1+1+1+1+1) > 15$.

Ah, there's something about the word synergy that has always hit me strongly. It's as if the word is greater than the letters that form it.

Jack Keenan

chapter 21
why, continued

People could ask, "If I wanted to have an intense, grueling experience, why wouldn't I just go join the Army and go to boot camp, and get *not just an adventure,* but a career. Rugby has been called civilized warfare, and there's no doubt that the adrenaline and survival instincts kick in during a game. There has been a growth of extreme sports, where people hop in a shopping cart, ride it down a hill, and then crash and fall out. Really, I've seen this on TV. And I've read about people who have combined rock-climbing and ironing. They reach the top of some rock pinnacle, and then they set up their ironing board and get steaming. I couldn't make this stuff up; I'm not that creative!

Philosophers and sociologists have debated about why people do these seemingly crazy things. Day to day life must not be exciting enough, that's my guess. We are lucky – indeed privileged – to not be confronted by matters of life and death on a daily basis. We lead far more comfortable lives than any other culture in history. We don't have to hunt for our food; we can just hit the local supermarket for almost anything that we need. With that comfort perhaps comes boredom. We must need something more. And, some of these things, I think we get from rugby: a sense of purpose in supporting the team, the satisfaction of a game well-played, camaraderie, and fun.

People play rugby because it is fun. Why else would anyone put in the time and effort, with the hours spent training in all kinds of weather, the costs involved with travel, and the constant physical battering? I can guarantee you that it is not for the fame and fortune, because neither exists here in the United States. I do guarantee you that everyone who is playing rugby is having fun. It's one of those things where, if you're *not* having fun, then you probably wouldn't have much incentive to keep playing.

Of course, I have used this argument at many points in my life. I used this argument to justify changing my major from chemical engineering to English my freshman year in college. I stood there in chemistry lab and asked myself, "Am I having fun?" The answer came back a resounding "no." And I didn't see it becoming fun in the future. So, an English major I became. Of course, that wasn't the last stop – or even a long stop – along my path of ever-changing majors.

chapter 22
anything she can do, I can do better!

Lest I forget, I should add that rugby players as a breed tend to be quite competitive. This pretty much goes without saying, but I thought I'd say it anyway.

Originally, this was a two-sentence chapter, but I now feel I must elaborate on this topic. Does rugby attract extremely competitive personalities? Or does rugby simply bring out one's latent competitive nature? It's another chicken and egg question. Which came first, the competitive environment of rugby, or the competitive personalities of those who play rugby? Did the sport help create the competitive personalities? Or, do competitive types gravitate towards sports like rugby?

As committed as the players are to their team, there is almost a higher commitment to the sport itself. Let me explain. Sometimes a team will show up with only 13 or 14 players. It's a pretty common practice for teams to loan a few players to an opposing team that shows up short-handed like this on the day of the game. What are the alternatives? If you play them 15 against 13 and win, then you haven't really proven anything. You had a built-in, automatic overload the whole game. And if you lose, it is a tough blow to your rugby honor, in that they were able to beat you while having fewer players. Now, sometimes, teams will play 13 against 13, or whatever. But, the emphasis is really on playing, and getting as many people who want to play out there on the pitch. So, you might be wearing the other team's jersey when you play, but at least you're playing. And as much as you want your team to win, you also want it to be a fair and decent match. So, even if you're playing for the other side, you still have to play the best you can. "Playing is the thing." I'm pretty sure that's what William Shakespeare meant to say.

Loaning players might seem inconsistent with the original statement that rugby players are competitive. At another level, it's about playing the best rugby you can, personally. It's in the spirit of that old adage, "whatever you do, do your best." And it's about both teams playing the best rugby possible, and "fighting the good fight." It's hard to improve without competition.

There is also competition within a team: for positions, playing time, and so on. Sometimes this sort of competition gets a bad rap. To put it in a more positive light, consider it this way: The team needs the best each player has to offer. We are never stronger than our weakest member.

There's a drill I recall doing at practice. First, groups of three are formed; these are your running buddies. The point is to run back and forth between some markers on the field as many times as possible within the allotted time limit. The first person runs up and back alone for the first lap, while the other two cheer. A second runner joins the first for the second lap. After the second lap, the first runner drops out to rest (and cheer) and runner three joins runner two for the next lap. After this lap, runner two drops out, and runner one joins runner three. And so on. At any given time, two people are running and one is resting (and cheering). Of the two people running, one is tired (from already having done a lap), and the other is fresh, and you get to alternate between these two conditions. And resting.

The new runner who joins in with fresh legs each time could easily leave her running buddy behind. But that's not what it's about. The idea is to pace your buddies, and to encourage them along. This drill is really about bringing each other along, because that's what you need to do in the game.

chapter 23
the great dichotomy

I believe that the rugby party tradition speaks volumes about the sport. It's what I call the great dichotomy. Two teams go out on a pitch, and for eighty minutes they battle each other as mortal enemies, tackling, pushing, driving each other as hard as they can. And then the last whistle blows, and they go have a drink up together. I know of absolutely no other sport that does this. Not a one.

When you're out on the pitch and playing the game, there is only one way to play, and that is with your whole heart, as if absolutely nothing else mattered. To quote a piece of wisdom that could be attributed to either Senator Eugene McCarthy or that wise sheriff of Mayberry, R.F.D., "You have to be smart enough to play the game, and dumb enough to think it matters." Senator McCarthy was comparing politics to football, and Sheriff Andy was talking to Opie about baseball, but the statement holds true across the board. What is play, in its simplest form, but this sort of suspended disbelief? When you're in the game, you buy into all the rules and regulations, the limits of the playing field, and the specified methods of accumulating points. And, most importantly, you believe that it matters.

The rugby party sits exactly 180 degrees opposite to this. It's the recognition that the final score doesn't really matter. Some players don't even know the final score when they step off the field. They may not even be completely sure who won! But they do know that there will be a party. It's the recognition that it all matters, and it all really doesn't matter, all at the same time. The party is not so much a celebration of winning, but of playing. After the game, the teams don't part and go their separate ways; they have a party together. You know your opponent in rugby. You may have even stayed at their house the previous night. Your opponent is not a faceless entity in rugby, but another living, breathing, flesh and blood human being. And there is a certain accountability and mutual respect that goes along with that knowledge.

chapter 24
amateurs

The sport of rugby in the US remains strictly amateur, although the laws were changed in 1997 to allow teams to accept corporate sponsorship to help defray team costs. The Super League was created that year, with the member teams selected from the existing field of men's teams. The number of teams and playoff format has changed slightly over the years, but it now consists of two 8-team conferences, with the top four teams going into post-season playoffs. The Super League is the closest thing we have to professional rugby here in the US. While sponsorship and fund-raising helps cover some team costs, certainly no one is being paid to play. No one makes a living in the US by playing rugby.

A new rugby venue is in the development phase: World Arena Rugby (WAR). It's similar to sevens, but would be played in a smaller, indoor arena, and would be complete with instant replays, cheerleaders and beer stands. And paid players. There is debate in the rugby community about whether this form of rugby may detract from the established game of fifteens. On the other hand, it can only increase the visibility of rugby in America. Hopefully, people will take home a favorable impression of the game, and maybe become more interested in the existing fifteens game.

Of the 120 rugby-playing nations, only the following have professional rugby teams: England, Wales, Ireland, Scotland, France, Italy, South Africa, Australia, New Zealand, and Argentina. With the exception of these teams, the overwhelming majority of the rugby players around the world are still amateurs. Even if a team obtains a local sponsor to help out financially, the amount of support typically does not come anywhere close to covering all the expenses involved, especially the travel. No one is giving up their day jobs any time soon. Just a handful of players from the US have moved abroad to pursue their dream of playing professionally.

According to Webster's, "amateur" can be defined in at least a couple of ways:

n. [Fr. < L. *amator,* lover < *amare,* to love]
1. a person who engages in some art, science, sport, etc. for the pleasure of it rather than for money; a nonprofessional; specifically, an athlete who is variously forbidden by rule to profit from his athletic activity
2. a person who does something without professional skill

Generally, where there are few pro teams in existence, it's not an issue of players lacking skill. So, we're looking at definition number one. In US rugby, there is actually very little hazard that players will profit from playing rugby. More likely, players will have accrued a pretty good credit card debt by the time they retire. Sometimes a team will try to provide job and housing contacts for a new player. Years ago, we joked about giving a $5 rugby scholarship at the University of Illinois. Things may be changing in this area now that some colleges are adding rugby as an official sport. Rugby scholarships of more than $5 could someday become a reality.

So, it is the first half of the first definition of amateur that applies: someone who plays rugby for the pleasure of it. The etymology of the word tells it all. It's French, derived from the Latin word, amator, meaning lover, which is from the root word, amare, to love. Amateurs play only for all the right reasons: the love of the game.

There's a verse that has been added to the song, "Bread of Heaven," that illustrates this point pretty well:

> We don't play for admiration,
> We don't play for victory.
> We just play for recreation,
> Fifteen fit rugby players are we!

We don't play for fame and fortune, that's for sure, as there is little fame or fortune to be had, outside of the occasional visit to the

White House. For the most part, the players are responsible for all the costs associated with traveling to away games and tournaments. I never thought twice about it when I was playing. I figured that youth happens once, and if I waited until I could afford to play, I'd be too old to play by then. It's all a matter of priorities. Some people spend their money on fancy cars, vacations, stocks, retirement funds, or other grown-up toys. Rugby players spend their money on rugby. It is no small commitment to play rugby, in terms of time, travel, money, and energy.

Most teams do a fair amount of travel during the season. And teams on the coasts probably do more than most. For example, within a single two-month season, Beantown might make a total of three or four trips to various destinations such as Washington D.C., Philadelphia, Atlanta, Chicago, and Minneapolis. That's only half the story, though; there's a fall season, too. California teams play from about November right through May. Canada teams play from about May through October. A lot of rugby gets played in the course of a year.

There are many administrative activities that go into directing the course of a team through the season: making sure that all the necessary forms are filed with USA Rugby, setting up the schedule a season in advance, sending in tournament entry fees, finding fields for practices and for games, collecting dues, making party preparations, making travel reservations, and ultimately, of course, playing. All of these duties are performed by the players. Typically, more than half the team members will hold some sort of office. Rugby teams are mostly autonomous – of, by, and for the players.

I remember schedules being handed out my first season, and I just figured some Rugby Schedule Board, similar to the NCAA or NFL, must have set up all the teams' schedules. Wrong! Each team's schedule is set up by its match secretary, who makes a bunch of phone calls to other match secretaries. In some areas, the match secretary is called the fixtures secretary; sounds like someone taking notes on the plumbing, but it's the same job.

Outside of a few league or territory matches that have to be played according to a particular schedule, a team has a lot of freedom to decide when and where to play the rest of the games in the season. Your team could decide to go on tour to England, California, or New Zealand, if you wished, and funds permitted. Needless to say, fundraising is pretty critical to the survival of a club.

I served as match secretary for both Illinois and Beantown for a couple of years each, where my job was to set up the best possible schedule for the team each season. The teams would have loved having home games the whole season, with at least two or three teams coming into town every weekend. That's not really practical, though, because we'd wind up owing everybody, and then our next season would be spent traveling every weekend. Mathematically, you wind up traveling more than you're home. If you have a couple of teams come to you on a given weekend, you then owe visits to both teams. So, it's inevitable that you're going to wind up traveling more than you're home.

Another team administrative duty is the selection process. Since most teams have more than fifteen players, and some may have enough players for two or even three sides, there has to be a way for a team to decide who plays which positions in each game. Most teams elect a selection committee (3 to 5 players typically). The coach(es) may or may not be on the selection committee. It depends on the team. When you vote for the Captain and the other selectors, you're investing your trust in those people to make the wisest decisions for the good of the entire team. Once the selectors have been elected, you abide by their decisions. It usually amounts to a democratically elected dictatorship on most teams. It doesn't always run smoothly, but it does get things done. It's never easy to tell a teammate that she hasn't been selected to play a certain game. Players ask "why?" And that's their right. The committee is accountable to the team.

The problem is that selections are complicated. People who play the same position will bring different things to the game physically, intellectually, and emotionally. You may have a shortage of people who play one position, and an overabundance at another position. There are a lot of different considerations. You need to give your rookies playing time, otherwise they won't learn the game, and they won't stick around. You also want to avoid overplaying someone ("you've been selected to play prop in the A-side, B-side, and C-side games today"). This can happen if you have a shortage of players who play a certain position. Selections may depend on the opponent's perceived strengths and weaknesses, the way that different combinations, or units, of players work together on the field, and what other games are scheduled for that day or weekend. Things can get extremely complicated at tournaments. It's a huge responsibility the team invests in its selection committee.

Sometimes selections are complicated by injuries. For example, the week before the 1996 Women's National Championships, Beantown's scrumhalf, Patty Connell, hurt her knee at practice. Scrumhalf is a pivotal position for a team, and Beantown was used to counting on Patty's levelheaded leadership on the field. What to do? If she played, she wouldn't be anywhere near 100 percent, and would risk turning a significant injury into a career-threatening one. Patty had to make a difficult decision. And I think it was a smart one. She sat out Nationals. That was probably one of the hardest things someone as competitive as Patty could ever do. Kerry Kilander McCabe, a flanker who hadn't played scrumhalf since her college days at Williams College, stepped into the position, and stepped up to the challenge with absolute grace and composure. It was just one of those things. In the face of what seemed like a crucial blow to the team's hopes of winning the championship, we could have fallen apart. But instead we pulled together, and won.

chapter 25
coaching

If rugby asks a lot from its players, it asks an even greater amount of dedication from those inspired individuals who answer the call to coach. Coaches expend a lot of time and energy planning and directing practice sessions during the week, and going to the games on the weekend. In many cases, the teams are self-coached, meaning that one or more player-coaches try to guide team strategy. That's the way it was at Illinois in the old days. Other clubs enjoy having an independent, objective coach on the sidelines to guide them. Some of the greatest rugby minds have helped guide the top-level teams to their success.

It may come as a surprise to some readers that a coach would have so much to worry about in terms of strategy. The way the game has been described so far, it probably sounds like poorly orchestrated chaos, at best. Believe it or not, there's a method to this madness, which sounds like something one of my grade school teachers used to say. Of course, William Shakespeare said it first: "Though this be madness, yet there is method in it."

I probably should have discussed rugby strategy many chapters ago, but if you play rugby, you already know what I'm talking about, and if you don't play rugby, even after reading this chapter, you still may have trouble identifying what the players are trying to do out there.

Strategy may mean different things to the forwards compared to the backs, but such strategies do in fact exist. The forwards are generally focused on obtaining, retaining, or advancing possession of the ball by doing forward-like things, such as rucks and mauls. In addition, the forwards can run plays off the scrums and lineouts (also referred to as set pieces, since they adhere to a certain structure, and occur after there has been a stoppage of play). And, sometimes a forward will – surprise! – join up with the back line. So you have that going on.

When I played at Illinois, though, the forwards generally had about three strategies that I was aware of: follow the ball, get the ball out to the backs, and stay out of the backs' way. So, we would run after the ball with all the enthusiasm of a pack of wild dogs chasing after a raw steak, which was kind of fun in that marauding mob kind of way. There are drawbacks to this approach, though, like having all 8 of your forwards stuck in a dog pile on one side of the field, while the ball has made its way out to the other side of the field. Like I said, these were the strategies I was aware of. In retrospect, I probably was not aware of all the information the coaches and other players were trying to share with me.

When I joined Beantown, I learned a number of things, such as: not everyone should go to the exact same place at the same time, and the backs do not always want the ball passed out to them. They only want the ball if they're set up, and they have room to run, and there's not a half dozen of the biggest opposition players inches from bulldozing them into the ground. Simple forward thinking: "The backs run faster. Give them the ball. They will make more yardage." Sometimes it is best for the forwards to keep the ball in the forward pack, rucking and mauling, until a clean ball can be produced for the backs.

Strategy for the backs can be boiled down to one thing: the two-on-one, also known as an overload. They may use any of a variety of tricks to get to this point. As the back line passes the ball out, they can skip one of the players, and move the ball farther out along the line, and upset the opposition's balance (the skip). Players can crisscross with each other (the switch), or, a player in the middle of the line, after passing off the ball, can run around to the end of the line (looping), or sometimes even just faking a pass (a dummy) can outwit the opponent.

The idea is to get more of our players running up the field with the ball against fewer of their players. It could also be a three-on-two, or a four-on-three. Each one of the defensive players can only effectively mark (be responsible for tackling) one of our players. So long as we somehow get an extra person out there, we should be able to break through their defense. Eventually, when it reaches the point where they have their last player trying to defend against two of ours, that individual will have to make a decision to commit to one player or the other. If the defensive player goes to tackle our ball carrier, then our player should pass the ball to her support. If the defensive player hangs out waiting for the pass, then the player with the ball may have a clear shot down the field.

It takes a bit of work to make these two-on-one situations happen, given that both teams each have fifteen players out on the field at all times. It involves making openings. Keep the ball in a ruck or maul, and get the other team to send too many players in to contest possession, then pass the ball out, and we should have some spare forwards out there on our side. Or, pass the ball one way to pull the defense that direction, and then send it back – quickly – the other direction. You may get a momentary overload as the opposing team's backs are out of position. These windows don't stay open forever. The moment is there, and then it's gone. You have to seize those opportunities when you can.

Rugby is a game that is both reactive and proactive in nature. Proactive in the sense that you have to go out and try to work your plays, strategies, and your game plan. You don't walk out on the pitch and just hope that things go your way. Rugby is also reactive in that you have to constantly adjust to the situation, and the situation is always changing. It's a moving target. We may have called a play to run the ball to the strong side of the field (the side the back line is set up), but a hole may have opened up weak (their wing has lost a shoe, whatever), so you take it weak instead. You have to be able to read the field, adapt and adjust to whatever happens out there, and communicate those changes effectively on the field.

chapter 26
Beantown's secret

Here in this chapter I will reveal to you Beantown's secret strategy responsible for the team's successful history. It's what has carried them to so many wins over the years, and has made them a respected member of the rugby landscape over the years. Right now, the players are saying, "Oh no! Rose is going to give away our secret! Wait a minute... What secret?" Well, it's not really that much of a secret.

Before every Beantown game, A-side, B-side or C-side, rain or shine, mud or snow, the whole team gets in a huddle and does the pre-game cheer. It's another rugby tradition. Some teams do silly, funny, nonsensical cheers, such as this one from my Illinois days:

Rick 'em, rack 'em, ruck 'em!
Come on team, let's go out and beat 'em!

Other teams do cheers to psyche themselves up and to intimidate the opponent. For example, New Zealand teams perform a traditional war dance of sorts, called the Haka, which can be traced back to the native Maoris.

For Beantown, the pre-game cheer forms the very foundation of the club's success, both on and off the field:

Go forward, support!

In this three-word cheer, however, lies the simplest, most fundamental, and profound strategy that Beantown tries to take into every game, and into every situation, every day, on and off the field.

Let's talk about "on the field" first. "Go forward, support" is the distillation of everything that goes into how the game of rugby is played. The cheer originated from the pre-game pep talk that the team's first captain, KO Onufry, would give the team. It's so hard to try to explain every detail of the game to a bunch of rookies in the five minutes before the whistle, especially with some of the twists of the laws. There's a lot of fine print. At Illinois, we would try to throw out reminders: "If you get tackled, you have to release the ball. If you score, touch the ball down. If the ball gets kicked out on the fly, and the kicker was behind their own 20-meter line, oh, never mind." Pretty soon it was just reduced to: "If we yell at you, don't take it personally, and we'll explain it after the game." This never got turned into a cheer, though.

Beantown was lucky enough to have KO, because in those last, final moments before the game, in trying to summarize everything that the players needed to do, she would always come back to those two concepts: go forward and support. When you boil down all the rules and all the strategies, this is the essence of the game.

Go forward. Don't run sideways. Don't run away from your supporting players. Run directly up the field. Confront the opposition, force them to commit, and use your best judgement to choose a course of action.

Support. When the play breaks down, get there to set up the ruck or maul, or get into good field position to take the pass coming off the ruck or maul. No one goes anywhere alone.

To play rugby, you need to have a certain level of fitness, and you need to develop good, sound, basic rugby skills. And you can have a coach and you can have some very neat and fancy plays. But every opponent is different, and every game starts with a blank scorecard. And when it comes right down to it, and everything's not quite clockwork, and you're right up against it, you've got to have something solid to fall back on. It's as much a game plan as it is a mental attitude. When all else goes awry, you can always come back to this: go forward, support. It's something you can hang your hat on. It's as simple as it is powerful, as the two are so often related.

It's a game plan that can be applied to just about any conceivable human relationship you might encounter. Going forward is about facing your problems, making decisions, and committing to them. Support is about dealing with the consequences of those actions, reevaluating the situation, making adjustments, and gathering strength to continue your forward motion. Support is critical in rugby because, as you recall, there is no blocking for the person with the ball. It's the same way in life. You can't shield people from life's challenges. All you can do is be there for them. There are different ways to support. Sometimes, it means rolling up your sleeves, joining right in, and helping someone, shoulder to shoulder. And, sometimes, it means staying at some distance, in a position of strength, to be ready to take the pass, and take up the charge. And sometimes, it's about bringing each other along the best you can, even if it means only yelling encouragement from the sidelines.

In rugby, there is often a tendency for players to run sideways with the ball, across the field, as the opposition draws near. When a player does this, though, not only are they running from the opposition, but also away from their own support players, making it harder for them to do their job.

We do this in everyday life sometimes. When we have problems, sometimes we isolate ourselves from our support networks. We try to take things on by ourselves. Yet, these are precisely the times that we need our support networks the most. Don't run away from your support. Sometimes this support is in a friend, a phone call, or a family member. And, sometimes it's in a therapist. Long before there were professional therapists, though, there were friends. People have always sought solace, comfort, and advice from a wide range of support networks.

Let's see how the go forward, support game plan works when applied to our first set of relationships: the family. Go forward. That babies grow up, that boys and girls become men and women, that we are all getting older every day – is incontrovertible fact. We are all going forward, whether we want to or not. Sometimes we're hurtling forth into the vast unknown. Other times, it feels like we're crawling through time. But it's always forward. And along the way, we encounter all sorts of life experiences – good, bad, and indifferent – and this is how we grow.

The family, ideally, is a stable platform from which its members venture out into the world, and to which they can return when they need to. Robert Frost put it far more eloquently in the poem, "Death of the Hired Man":

> Home is the place where, when you have to go there,
> They have to take you in.

No matter what you do, your family is your family. There's no return or exchange window for this item. It's a package deal, and it's for life.

Certainly, over the years, marriages seem to have become less stable. Less permanent. Why is this? I was at my eighth grade class reunion (we do these things back in the Midwest), and I asked several people what they thought. One woman said, "It's because people aren't committed. They don't really think about what 'for better and for worse' means." She's probably right. But, if everyone really thought about just how bad the "for worse" part could be, then no one would probably ever get married. But we do. We go forward. But, maybe we don't know how to support as well as we could. We hit opposition, and we give up. We're *not* there for each other.

chapter 27
when things don't go as planned

"Go forward, support." The most basic principles of the game. When you go out on the field, you need to have a plan; you need to know who is playing what positions, which plays you're going to run, and what your overall strategy is. And you need a philosophy to go back to when things *don't* go as planned: go forward, support.

It is my premise that life is a lot like rugby. There are no guarantees; nothing is a given. Sometimes the best-laid plans go awry, and sometimes Serendipity smiles on a rainy day. You don't always get four quarters for your dollar. Sometimes you get more, and sometimes less. The best team doesn't always win. And the rules are always changing.

The frailty of human plans in light of the greater powers-that-be is captured in a saying Reverend Mychal Judge, New York Fire Chaplain, was known for: "Want to know how to make God laugh? Tell him what you're going to do tomorrow." There is so much that is beyond our control. Reverend Judge was one of the first to die that fateful September day.

We all hear people say that life is unfair. It's hard to define exactly what fair is. There are so many of us here with our lives all interconnected and intertwined. What's good for one may not be good for another. Let's say it rains. Somebody's boat goes down in the storm, and somebody's crops are saved. For there to be a winner, there has to be a loser. That's what we're taught. A lot of things just happen, though. They are what they are. The judgment part, whether something is labeled good or bad, hinges on how we are affected as individuals. And yet, we will never know the net impact of all the repercussions, echoes, and ripples emanating from a single event. Outcomes can run quite counter to the intended results.

A lot of people hang their hat on religion. If we can't be guaranteed a fair shake in this life, it's nice to believe that justice will be meted out in the next life. But, even if your faith is strong, let's face it: This life can be hard. Can you live your entire life simply looking forward to getting your just rewards at the Pearly Gates when it's all over? Is the fear of the afterlife enough to get people to be nice to each other every day? Obviously not. Isn't there any present-day worth to being good and decent? Or is it all in futures, as the stockbrokers would say.

How do we deal with the present? How do we live today? It's easy to be practically overwhelmed by the randomness of it all sometimes. Read the newspaper on any given day, and you'll find half a dozen stories. The story of the 18-wheeler that hurtled off the interstate in Hartford, landing on a little pickup truck 80 feet below. Both guys walked away from the wreckage with only minor injuries. Yet, two people were killed on another interstate when a small airplane crashed into their station wagon. What are the odds of that? It's so random. It can all seem pretty meaningless when you realize that no matter what you do, some things are just going to go their own way, no matter what you do. If that's the case, then why even try?

I asked myself a lot of these questions after I walked away from a minor motorcycle crash. The bike was totaled. My friend and I could have been totaled. But we weren't. We crashed into the cornfield, and not one of the telephone poles. That simple. You'd think that I would have just been happy to be alive at that point. It doesn't happen that fast, it's not s straight-line path. I mostly thought about how I could just as easily have died. This experience just illuminated for me the very randomness of it all. And the fragility of life. This weighed on me for quite a while, until one day it occurred to me: So, the price of having good times is just not knowing how long they'll last. You can either sit around waiting for the cloud of doom to approach, or you can enjoy the good times that you have. Yes, life is fragile, and it can be taken away in the flash of a moment. But, it's the only thing we can really call our own, so we'd better give it our best shot. When you get the chance to grab some of those good times, grab on tight, and enjoy them, for you know not how long they've come to stay.

The recent Columbia shuttle tragedy brought up memories of when the Challenger exploded just seconds after liftoff. Who can forget those images? Both tragedies came as such a shock. Who could look at the tape of the Challenger explosion, played over and over, and not think, "There were people up there in that blast of smoke and flame; people we just saw last night on the news in our living rooms." They had been so excited, so alive. They had so wanted to do this mission. I'm sure none of them wanted it to turn out the way it did, but they were aware that there were certain risks associated with any space mission. And they must have accepted that.

There are countless other tragic accidents and twists of fate that defy rationale explanation or understanding. As long as planes have flown, planes have fallen out of the sky. There is nothing that is completely safe, either in nature or the man-made world. Even if you never venture out, there are the various diseases that prey on us from within.

None of us really get to choose how we die, but we do get to choose how we live.

Life is dangerous. And yet, it seems like there are two options: Either play ball, or take your boots off and go home. The only problem is that, once you decide to play the game, you also have to accept all the rules that go along with this game. If you play, anything can happen. If you play, you might get hurt. If you don't play, you'll never win, and you still may get hurt.

This life is the most precious thing that we own. We can either keep it safe on a shelf, or we can take it out and work with it, to make it into what it is meant to be.

Oscar Wilde put it this way: "Life is too important to be taken seriously." Really, life is simply too important not to be lived.

go forward, support!

Charles River (photo/rs)

chapter 28
the stone in the stream

In rugby, teams often must deal with the unexpected. Any player could get injured, and be forced to leave the game at any time. One missed tackle, or a kick picked up by the wrong player, and the opponent could suddenly be a meter away from scoring, and your team backed up against the try line. A comfortable lead could be erased by a sudden shift in momentum. A team could call and cancel the match the day before the game. Any number of variables – injuries, the wind, the referee, the opponent, traffic on the way to the game – can affect the team.

How we deal with these twists of fate reflect greatly on our internal bearings.

Have you ever watched a stream or a brook? It's not always immediately apparent which way the stream is flowing. You can't always tell just by watching the water. Unless there's a stone in the stream. By watching the way the water hits the stone (or other obstacle) and moves around it, you would be able to tell which way the current is flowing.

Maybe this is how our lives work. Maybe it matters *most* how we deal with the obstacles in our lives; the things that *don't* go as planned. When the current hits an obstacle, such as the stone, it has to react to it, find a new way around it or over it, ultimately moving beyond it. In the process, the water changes its shape, giving physical evidence of the direction in which it is moving.

I like the stream metaphor for life. Always moving forward (downstream), and dealing with the obstacles in its path. How we deal with our obstacles gives tangible evidence of our underlying character. These are often the defining moments in our lives. So, in some fashion, we could look at these obstacles as *opportunities* to prove ourselves; to test our mettle, to show what we're made of. Or, as Ralph Waldo Emerson put it:

> What lies behind us and what lies before us are tiny matters, compared to what lies within us.

A stream that has no obstacles in its path is still flowing. In the same way, a person who has never had to face a particular problem may have the strength and fortitude to deal with it, but they've just never had to prove it. They've not been tested.

Even if you haven't personally faced much in the way of adversity, you can still pose any number of "what-if" questions to yourself. Coming up with the answers to these questions can be a very instructive exercise. Writer Eudora Welty also recognized the importance of the internal workings:

> A sheltered life can be a daring life as well.
> For all serious daring starts from within.

It's also likely that the more obstacles you must deal with, the better you become at dealing with obstacles in general. Nietzsche popularized this concept: "That which does not kill us, makes us stronger." Not only does it make us stronger, I think it makes us more human. Or, at least, more capable of appreciating what it is to be human. The human condition is such an imperfect condition. And sometimes we forget that. Not for very long, usually, as reminders are quick and sure to appear, whether we want them to or not. It's not all bad. It's a mixed bag, this business of being human. And, mostly, it is what it is.

The more experiences we have – triumphs, defeats, and all the draws in between – the more planes on which we'll be able to relate to our fellow humans who have had similar experiences. So, we are all building up our libraries of experiences; volumes and volumes of "what it is to be human." A giant database. That's one way to look at it. It has always helped give me some perspective, recognizing that I'm not the first person ever to have gotten a flat tire or a speeding ticket. Not the first to break a heart, and not the first to have my heart broken. Not the first person to score a 4 on the Calculus midterm. Yes, that's a 4 percent. Four points out of 100. (I got partial credit on one of the problems.)

Well, okay, maybe I am alone on that last one. But, surely, somebody else out there got a 5? Maybe a 3? No? Well, that's okay because I still got a good story out of it. Wasn't that a great story? (I will take your silence as agreement.)

Before we leave the analogy of the stone in the stream, there is something that must be pointed out. While it may seem that the stream is simply moving around the stone, it is very slowly but surely, if imperceptibly, wearing away at the stone. Water is perhaps the single most powerful erosive agent on our planet. Given enough time, the stream will wear a rock down to sand grains. If you don't have a hammer, but you have time and patience, persistence will serve you well.

So, when I re-took Calculus, I tried a new approach. I worked every single problem at the end of every chapter. I ground my way through Calculus, problem by problem, for three semesters. And passed with flying colors. Of course, I can't remember a bit of it anymore, except that the derivative of x squared is 2x. The ironic thing is that I have never really used Calculus since I got out of school. Yet, at the time, it had seemed so very important to me, such a reflection on myself. There's a good lesson to come out of this:

Poetic Interlude #4

Objects in the mirror
Are closer than they appear.
And problems in the now
Seem much larger than they are.

chapter 29
decisions, decisions, decisions

If you decide to play the game, you buy into all the rules that go along with it, and you suspend disbelief, by believing that the game matters. You care about things, and that can make it much harder to make decisions.

When you come up against obstacles and forks in the road, you have to make decisions about how to get through them. These can be hard decisions to make. What's the right answer? Is there only one right answer? I don't think so. There are always many options. Some choices may appear preferable to others. But, the net effect of any given decision on the entire cosmos is impossible to know. Agonizing over these decisions can lead to paralysis, a halt to progress. We must go forward.

Decision-making should be viewed as another opportunity: the opportunity to exercise your free will. It's the chance to exert some degree of control over your own life, whether it's the colors of your walls, your dinner entrée or the direction of your career. There is an important link between this sense of control, self-esteem, and optimism, as explored in books, such as *Learned Optimism*, and *What You Can Change And What You Can't*, by Dr. Martin E. P. Seligman. This is important because such attitudes can become self-fulfilling prophecies. Optimists generally have better coping skills, and are able to keep trying despite initial failures. Optimists often lead happier lives. It is Dr. Seligman's premise that, in some areas, people can change the way they view the world. The human psyche has some flexibility to it. Some things are not so easily changed, but to some degree, optimism can be learned. Based on Dr. Seligman's approach, one of the keys to optimism is the feeling that one has some control over the positive things in one's life, that success is not a fluke. By the same token, it's important to recognize that failure is not always deserved, but sometimes just bad luck, and thus not a reflection of merit. One of the most important questions is this: How is it that we define our lives – by our successes or by our failures?

Decision-making is the opportunity to more clearly define what matters. Sometimes you may not even know the order of your priorities yourself, until you've been faced with these decisions to make. It's a way to get to know yourself better, to know what your values are, and what has meaning in your life.

In rugby, there is the concept of over-committing. If a ruck or maul forms, and they send in four players and we send in seven, then we have over-committed to that piece of the game. The other team now has three extra players running around out there, capable of inflicting damage against us because we don't have players to mark them. Even if we win the ball, we still won't have a good chance at getting an overload, as their extra players will be out there to break up any play that we attempt to run. We need to send only the necessary number of players into each piece.

The same is true in life. There are plenty of things that seem to demand our attention. It's easy to lose our focus, and get scattered. But if we devote our energy to unworthy causes, we won't have energy left for the things that really do matter to us. A good argument could be made for the judicious use of apathy towards things that are not really deserving of our attention, so that we can reserve our best for the things that matter to us most. And that is at the very heart of it. What is it that really matters? What is it that makes life worth living? And how closely do our day-to-day activities mirror our actual values and priorities?

Viktor Frankl provides a stirring examination of some of these very questions in his book, *Man's Search for Meaning*. He is a survivor of the Holocaust, an experience beyond any that most of us could ever imagine, and one that no human being should ever have had to endure. Stripped of absolutely everything and everyone that had mattered to them, and constantly placed on death's threshold, some of the Holocaust prisoners found within themselves an internal meaning to their lives, which gave them a reason to get through each day. Stripped of everything, all that remained was whatever hope they could create for themselves. Dr. Frankl calls this "tragic optimism": the ability to make the best of things in the face of tragedy, when all that is left is "what lies within."

Dr. Frankl might not agree with Dr. Seligman about the ability to self-generate optimism. The basis of his logotherapy approach is that, to be optimistic, you would need something to give you a reason for feeling that way. Dr. Frankl would counsel us to look for those reasons, those things that define the meaning in our lives. The reasons for living.

It's very moving to read Dr. Frankl's account of his time at the concentration camp. What seemed to help him endure the experience was the love he felt in his heart for his wife. She was not there with him, in fact, she had already died, but he did not know that. His love for her transcended time, space, and death, and gave him meaning in his life. Love is undoubtedly the single-greatest reason for living.

chapter 30
"I look back on my life…"

Sometimes, when we're looking back on our lives, and the decisions we've made, we are bound to have a few regrets. In an ideal world, we'd never have any regrets. We'd always do the right thing. As we all learn, though, life is not simple. We face hard decisions. Sometimes we have to make compromises. Even once we've made up our minds to pursue a particular course of action, it may not be so easy to implement that decision. And then we have to live with the choices we've made. It's easy to be hard on oneself. "D'oh!" as Homer Simpson would say. We're stuck with being human, and all that entails.

Things don't always go as we would like. Problems come up. "Things fall apart, it's scientific." That's the way David Byrne and the Talking Heads put it in "Wild Wild Life." We all make mistakes. And where do most problems crop up? At the seams. At least that's what my carpet installer told me. And it's true for a lot of other things, too. It's where the rubber meets the road, and where the river meets the sea. It happens between individuals, states, and nations. It happens in factories, families, at work, and at play. Any place where two things meet, that's where the potential for problems is greatest. The Challenger tragedy was traced back to a faulty O-ring seal at a connection.

We also have the most to learn from such seams and boundaries. A lot of interesting things happen there. They happen because all the differences between the parties are magnified at these contacts. Often, what should be seamless simply isn't.

Let me digress for a moment. How does an earthen dam fail? Two ways, either by overtopping or by internal seepage and erosion of material through the dam. Dams don't start to fail across their entire length, they fail as a result of either the water getting too high, or the water finding a pathway, a crack or a seam of more pervious material.

People, too, don't usually fail throughout their very being. We fail when the water gets too high. And we fail through the small breaks and seams in our character. It's the little things that pull us down. "Character flaws," the English teachers would call them. Most people are not inherently, pathologically evil, we're just flawed. Yet, these flaws, given the opportunity, can bring the whole person down.

In the song, "Watershed," by the Indigo Girls, there's the line, "every five years or so I look back on my life and I have a good laugh." When you look back, it may be hard to laugh at some parts of it. Some people are racked with guilt or regret. They can't forgive themselves for what they've done, and they can't get beyond that. I understand this, being somewhat of a perfectionist by nature. I'm human, and therefore bound to make mistakes. Sometimes the hardest thing is forgiving yourself for your own failings and imperfections and mistakes; forgiving yourself for being human.

Sometimes, when I'm looking back with some regret, I try to re-visit myself *as I was then*, when I was faced with tough decisions. I try to picture myself, 5 or 10 or 15 years ago. What were my dreams, my fears, my hopes, and my passions? What was driving me at that time?

Imagine going and sitting down next to yourself – at school, at work, on the bus, at a bar, a diner, or some other favorite old haunt. Imagine looking at yourself with all the wisdom you have acquired since that time. Things are so clear in retrospect. Half the things you worried about then probably never materialized. Then, there are the other things you probably never saw coming that completely blindsided you. "What we anticipate seldom occurs; but what we least expect generally happens," British author and statesman Benjamin Disraeli (1804-1881) was quoted as saying.

Our lives and our selves are constantly changing, evolving. Certainly, I am not the same person I was ten years ago. None of us are. I guess that's another reason why I like to keep a journal – it's a good reality check, a way to ground truth my memories. It's amazing how much we tend to forget, both by accident and design. There's a saying among the retired rugby players: The older we get, the better we were. Memory can be a slippery thing. And sometimes, looking back, patterns emerge that would never have been apparent in the myopic vision of the present.

The journal-keepers I've met (myself included), as a breed, seem compelled to try to capture the thoughts and feelings of the present day. And, sometimes things just crystallize perfectly, the words flow and make sense, and you just nail it. It's so much more than just a record of events; it's the story of a life.

Eudora Welty, one of the great storytellers, spoke also of feeling this "need to hold transient life in *words* – there's so much more of life that only words can convey." A journal provides one a tiny window for viewing one's former selves

One woman, in an interview reported in *USA Today* (May 15, 1997), spoke of her memories of the painful breakup of a relationship she had been in years ago.

> I kept a journal at the time, and not too long ago, (after) reading it, I sat in my closet and wept for the woman I used to be.

And who was that woman? Oprah Winfrey.

When I re-visit myself like this, I also get a sense of the vulnerability of my former selves. I have learned to have a little more respect and compassion for all of who I've been. It also reminds me of the potential for what lies ahead. Sometimes I think, I probably haven't even met some of the most important people of my life yet. I know this statement would have been true five years ago. Why wouldn't it be true today?

As much as this exercise in time travel provides some insight on how to live with myself, it also has taught me much about showing other people the same respect and compassion for who they are today. If you can't show forgiveness and compassion to a former self, how will you forgive other people and accept them, flawed, as the humans they are? You have to be able to forgive yourself as well as others. It has often been said that you can't truly love another person until you love yourself. To love is to forgive, to accept another's human-ness.

Some of the most important people you ever forgive may be those who never sought or asked for your forgiveness. Does love really mean never having to say you're sorry? Or was that only true in the movies (*Love Story*). Maybe love is also sometimes saying, "You're forgiven," even when no one has said they're sorry. They may not even be sorry. They may not be capable, physically or emotionally, of apologizing. But, they don't have to be sorry for you to forgive them. You may not actually put it in words to the person, but if it happens in your heart, then it is real. You have that power within you.

Why would someone seek your forgiveness in the first place? It's usually because you've been hurt in some way, knowingly or unknowingly, by someone. Forgiving is not denying that the hurt occurred, but acknowledging the human condition. Forgiving someone lets you put it behind you, and to move forward. It's about loving yourself, and putting more energy into the future, rather than letting the past have the power to control you.

Poetic Interlude #5

Watercolor Riverstrings

People are rivers
pasts flowing into presents
into futures
like watercolors mixing.

Emotional strings
don't come unattached.

She pushed her,
but she didn't push back.
Why?

Because I knew
not to fight her, see -
sometimes she just goes off -

You mean, goes off the deep -

Yeah, off the deep end,
maybe because
of what her dad
did to her
when she was a kid.

Watercolor riverstrings -
when will they end?

rs

chapter 31
indispensability vs. disposability

Every job I have ever had, sooner or later, someone eventually gives the "No-one-is-indispensable" speech. It was true 15 years ago, and it's just as true today. There are both up-sides and down-sides to this statement. At my first real job, they tried to make it sound like, "We're a team here. Don't feel like you have to take everything upon yourself. We can all share the load." That's what the optimists heard. The rest of the room heard, "We can survive quite well and fine without any one of you. You're all replaceable." I don't think most workers want the burden of being indispensable, though, either. It's nice for a while, maybe, but it would get tiresome. Most workers probably just want to fall somewhere in-between, in that zone of feeling somewhat useful and needed. It's quite a simple concept, but one that corporate America has often failed to grasp.

Let's face it. All anyone ever really wants – whether it's at work, at home, or anywhere – is to feel that they matter. That what they put their energy into has some meaning. That their life has some meaning. It's a key element to all relationships. People needing, and being needed by other people.

I was talking to an old classmate who had been through a couple of divorces. When asked why he thought marriages didn't stay together, he said, "It seems like some people believe relationships are disposable. If they don't like the old one, they just get a new one." By the same token, it's probably not healthy for one to define oneself purely by one's relationship with another person. It's too much to ask of the other person. It puts them in the "indispensable" category. Healthy is probably somewhere between these two extremes.

Is there such a thing as a disposable relationship? It can happen. Your path crosses with that of a stranger. You doubt you'll ever meet again. Why be kind or civil to that person? What's the motivation? Is there one?

Our paths go all over the place. You never know when or how paths may cross again. The way the world works, it would be very difficult to completely isolate oneself. We depend on some people for some things, and others depend on us for other things. We are all interconnected, our lives intersecting and touching one another's, like the infinite interactions of ripples on a pond as each raindrop lands. We are all related. Interrelated. No person is an island. It's a small world that just keeps getting smaller.

Think about the game of rugby. First of all, when I think about all the people I have played rugby with and against, I realize that, by proxy or by so many degrees of separation, I have probably played with or against practically every woman rugger in the US and a few foreign countries. No woman is an island.

Secondly, there is an elementary need for other players and teams. Does it mean anything to run down the field with the ball and touch it down – if you're the only one on the field? I don't think so. The rugby world is another interactive system. What's the use of being the best player at a certain position if you don't have a team to play on? What's the use of having a rugby team if there are no other teams to play? We need our opponents as much as we need our teammates. It's how we get better – by playing and testing our skills against the opposition. There are some great rivalries in the rugby world, and these have contributed greatly to the continuing improvement in the level of play for all teams involved. It's important to keep a healthy respect for the opponent. Certainly, never underestimate them.

Poetic Interlude #6

<u>Two Doors Down</u>

You work at the Donut Shoppe
on Mattis Avenue
where I do my laundry
two doors down.

I don't know you
but I met your grandma
at a rest stop
restaurant
and we started talking
until we found
some common ground.

rs

chapter 32
what's your job?

We are all needed, then, to serve some vital function in the grand overall scheme of things. Whatever that is. Which brings me to one of my favorite stories. This took place before I joined Beantown, so it's actually coming to you second or third hand.

One night, our coach, Kevin, was running a practice session, and he had the players split up into teams. The two sides were playing against each other, to simulate the game situation. Apparently, they were trying to work some plays, and things just weren't going quite right. Kevin was getting more and more frustrated, and he finally called the players in for a discussion.

"What is your job?" he asked. It seemed like a pretty basic question, really, but people had a hard time coming up with the answer he was looking for.

Finally, when the right answer wasn't forthcoming, Kevin gave up.

"No, no, no," he said.

"Your job is: to *know* what your job is!"

chapter 33
what are we doing here?
(or: what are we here to do?)

Sometimes when I'm pondering this age-old question, I think of that Kevin story. And then I wonder if the answer isn't in the very asking of the question. Maybe we're here just to figure out why we are here.

Does anyone remember the Rubik's Cube? You could twist a layer of the colored blocks along any of the three axes. After just a few twists and turns like this, the cube quickly became a mess of multi-colored panels. The point of the puzzle was to get it back to its original condition, with each face of the cube all the same color. "Over three billion combinations... just one solution," reads the package.

Sometimes I think our lives are like messed up Rubik's Cubes. We're handed them at birth, and told to figure them out. The thing about our puzzles is that they're constantly changing, and they're intertwined with other peoples' puzzles. Every move you make in your puzzle somehow affects other peoples' puzzles. And, unlike Rubik's Cube, there's no one right solution, but still over three billion combinations.

To continue with this analogy, one could ask about the equality of peoples' puzzles. I'd say that we're all equal in the sense that we are all born with one of these puzzles. We will all have things to sort out in this lifetime.

"There will be happy days and sorry days," as my father has always said. "And you have to learn to live with both." But, one could argue that some puzzles are easier than others. Or, to refer back to an earlier analogy, some people have more stones in their stream. Right from the get go. Undeniably, the individual set of circumstances that you are born into will define certain aspects of your life.

When I was a little kid, maybe five or six years old, I remember thinking about what made people different. It was all a matter of where you were born. It wasn't anyone's fault they were born rich or poor, or black, brown, or white. What if anyone could have been born into any family anywhere? What if, before we're born, our souls hang around up in the heavens, waiting for our turn to be born? I call this my Deli Counter Theory of Souls. There couldn't be any sense of superiority or entitlement due to class, race, or skin color, because any one of us could have been born in someone else's place. The concept of a birthright flies right out the window.

So, there's what you're born with, and there's what you pick up along the way. One's early life experiences will likely shape how one perceives the world, and judges one's self-esteem. Is the world a happy and safe place? Or is it a fearful place?

Vast differences exist in the realm of human experiences. Yet, I would never get into the business of trying to quantify the impact of the difficulties of one life compared to another. It seems like one's problems and despair expand to fill the space that one allows for them. It's impossible to know what pains have been experienced in a person's life, unless you have walked the proverbial mile in their shoes. Or played a season in their cleats. This is all the more reason to restrain ourselves from judging others too quickly or too harshly; to look on others with some compassion. And to remember, "there, but for the grace of God, go I." These words were first spoken by John Bradford in the 1500s, and are just as true today.

There was a TV show called "Quantum Leap," which ran between 1989 and 1993, and you can still catch reruns of it on some channels. The main character not only travels back through time, but also travels into a different person's body each time that he leaps. Each episode begins with our hero, Dr. Sam Beckett (played by Scott Bakula), landing in the middle of someone's life and trying to figure out exactly who this person is and why he is there. Usually, he's there to effect some change in the course of events that will have far-reaching impacts on the course of history, or at least on the lives of the individuals involved. And sometimes not. One episode, his purpose was simply to cure a sick pig. He thought he was there to fall in love with the owner of the pig, a damsel in distress. In the end, his guide (with the help of a computer named Ziggy) confirms what his purpose was, and provides feedback on how the future has been changed. We are not privy to such information in our own lives. On the other hand, we only have one life to figure out and we get an entire lifetime (instead of sixty minutes) to work on it. Imagine: If Scott Bakula leapt into your life today, what would he think his/your purpose was? Of course, we have no Ziggy, and we never get clear confirmation of what we're here to do. All we have is our best judgement to go on. It's important to ask the question, though. It's easy to become complacent. Time has a funny way of flying when you don't keep an eye on it. Who wants to wake up someday to find that some of your greatest hopes and dreams were never realized, and worse, never even attempted?

There was a song that came out in the eighties, by Joe Jackson: "You can't get what you want, till you know what you want." As simple as that may be, it is also true.

Sometimes we don't even know what we want. We keep a lid on our expectations. That way we won't be disappointed too often. It's an eye-opening exercise, however, to take some time out, and let yourself go wild, and really think about all the things you might like to do. Natalie Goldberg describes a similar exercise in her book, *Writing Down the Bones*, in a chapter titled, "What are your deep dreams?" We are defined not only by what we actually accomplish, but also by our aspirations, the things that drive us.

No matter how crazy, unrealistic, or preposterous some of your dream goals may sound, you'll find out a lot about what's going on inside of you. That some of these things may never actually come to fruition may not matter so much as what you learn about yourself in the process, in the very asking of the question. The things on your list speak volumes about the person you are. In the process, you may find that there are one or two items that you seriously want to pursue.

Once you've picked a dream to pursue, write it down on paper, and then try to picture yourself actually doing it. Fill it in with all the details. If you can see yourself doing something, you're that much closer to being able to do it. It no longer seems so improbable. Visualization is a tried and true tool of both athletes and artists alike.

How do you decide which dreams to follow? One must decide which things matter most to them, and prioritize their lives accordingly. We all face difficult decisions, and I have absolutely no magic advice to offer. We can't let such indecision paralyze our lives, though. Yes, things need to matter, but not so much that we're afraid to take a step in either direction. We must go forward. All we can do is do our best. We're not here to lead perfect lives; we're here to live human lives, which tend to be far more interesting.

Poetic Interlude #7

<u>The Local Purity World</u>

Monday night is hell
at the local Purity World:
all those shoppers
with their shopping baskets full.

All our wants
our needs
that they could all be filled
from some well-stocked shelf
at the Purity World Supreme!

rs

Note: The Purity World Supreme was a local grocery store chain in the Boston area. The stores were bought out by Stop & Shop in 1995.

chapter 34
hope at the hardware store

Every season brings new hope to a team. Teams set goals and talk about what they'd like to do better this season: dominating the scrum, working the back plays, etc. And scoring more points than the opponents!

How else would a team go into a season? "Last year was good, but let's take it down a notch this year." Whatever a team may have experienced the previous season, the new season represents a fresh slate, a time to start all over again.

The resiliency of the human spirit is an amazing thing. It's hard to believe sometimes, the stories one hears about people being knocked down over and over again, and still being able to pick themselves up. Hope is one of those strange organisms that exists merely at the thought that it exists. After all, if you believe there is hope, then you have hope! It is self-generating.

What is hope?

Sometimes hope is a weed, with long, woody roots, that won't go away. Sometimes hope is a stray dog that you've fed too many times, and now it keeps you awake at night, barking at your door.

And sometimes hope is a hardware store. It can be the little, jammed-shelf neighborhood shop, or one of the newer Home Depot type warehouses. Hardware stores are full of *potential*. They *smell* of potential. Wood, paint, caulking, grout, tile. And all the tools and gadgets and everything you need to get stuff done. To make things better.

There's often a wonderful sense of camaraderie at the hardware store. Everyone is shopping, deciding what they want, and what they need to get the job done. The right tools and the raw materials.

Some are in crisis-mode, responding to urgent repair needs: faulty plumbing, broken windows, leaky roofs, and the like. The rest are there with projects in mind. To put up nicer wallpaper, or to put down better flooring. To shim up what's tilting, or to replace what's worn. Better. Not perfect, necessarily. Just better. But, better is a good thing.

Even in our darkest hours, when nothing seems to be going right, we somehow manage to keep on going. What is it that pulls us, or pushes us forward, if not just the belief that things might get better? To hope is human. If everybody truly believed that the world was such a horrible place, and that nothing would ever get better, no one would ever get married, have children, plant trees, sing songs, or write poems. Or go to the hardware store.

chapter 35
hope is in a tree

I think we could learn some lessons from trees. What do trees do, but take in materials (sunlight, water, air, and nutrients from the soil), and then process these materials into new growth: roots, branches, stems, and leaves. They shoot straight up out of the ground, seeking the sun, absolutely plumb with the pull of gravity, balanced in the tension between sun and earth, and always growing. Just as we have certain things in our lives that we can't change, trees also live within certain constraints. They grow where they are planted. And when conditions change, they too must either adapt or perish. If we can imitate the trees, we'll be doing well. Take in all the experiences that life throws at you, process them, and grow. That sounds like a pretty good formula.

Poetic Interlude #8

What an important job
trees have –
holding up the sky
and changing the seasons.

Have you ever really looked at the bark of a tree? It's rough, hard, dry and craggy. It has to be, to protect the stuff inside from the elements. For within the tree, there are soft, wet, woody fibers carrying water and nutrients up to the leaves and branches, just as surely as a beating heart. People are like trees in this way. Sometimes people also grow a crusty shell to protect them from the outside elements, but it doesn't mean that there's no life or joy within. There is that within all of us.

Poetic Interlude #9

Boats

what are boats
but trees
that have gone to sea?

tethered with ropes
and set with sail
to catch the every breeze

and what is the wind
but what comes and goes
always and again?

rs

chapter 36
weighted and naked

There are days, and then there are days. Some days I wish I could just "take a minute." In the middle of a busy day, stuck in traffic, or just rushing around trying to do too much in a day. Just sixty seconds to pause, catch my breath, shake things off, and make sure that I've still got it all together.

I suspect that the injury minute evolved pretty early in the history of rugby. Sometimes, you take a pretty hard hit, and you wonder if you're still in one piece. Most of the time, you just need a minute to check it out, tape it up, shake it off, and get back in the game. Sometimes, though, a player comes off the field limping, or holding a collarbone that is in more pieces than it ought to be. Once you leave the game, you're not allowed back in, with one exception. A temporary sub is allowed for a player who is merely bleeding, so they can leave the field, staunch the flow of blood, clean it up, cover it up, and return to the field.

So, do people ever play when they're injured? Sometimes, probably. Do people play rugby when in pain? Often. It's a tough sport. When you play rugby, you know that you're going to be hitting the ground, and taking hits, and tackling other players in the course of a game. You can't play rugby and expect not to get a few cuts and bruises along the way. When you step out on the field, you recognize that there are risks in playing the game. You know that you might get hurt. You train and you practice, and you do everything you can to reduce the chance of serious injury. But things do happen.

I was at the gym one day, doing some weightlifting. I'm still working on getting my right shoulder back into shape. I apparently separated it (very slightly) one season, and it has bothered me a little bit ever since. Of course, it didn't bother me enough to go see a doctor for several months. Eventually, I did get myself to a sports thera-pist, and started on a training program to start rehabilitating the muscles around the shoulder. If you saw me at the gym, you wouldn't know that I have this old injury. I can lift a respectable amount of weight for someone my size (i.e., small). But I know it's there. I adjust for it. I've cut out some exercises, and added others to make up for it.

How different is all of this from everyday life? Do people "play" with injuries? Do people keep playing even when they're in pain? The answer would have to be yes. Isn't society full of the walk-ing wounded? I don't mean just the physical pains, ills, scars, and injuries. What about the emotional scar tissue on people's psyches? Battle wounds, scraped knees, and bruised hearts. Nietzsche was only half right. Sometimes that which doesn't kill you makes you stronger, and sometimes that which doesn't kill you only leaves you damaged, injured, and weakened.

Yes, I'd say we all play injured. For better or worse, we bring with us all the baggage – physical, emotional, intellectual, cultural – we've accumulated so far. We go into every day with the weight of all that has passed before us resting on our shoulders.

Weighted. And yet naked.

Naked as the day we first entered this world. Naked in the sense that this is a new day that has never been lived before. A clean slate, a blank canvas, pure unspoiled potential.

Just because your team won the National Championship last year does not mean that you'll win it again this year. There are no guarantees. Going into this year's tournament, though, you will have the benefit of all the lessons learned and experiences gained from last year's victorious tournament. All of those lessons and experiences are stored away in the heart, mind, body and soul. It's like the basketball player shooting a free throw, or the tennis player delivering a serve. It's as if their body has memorized the pattern of movements, from just the right stance, to the release and follow through. Muscle memory.

All of our experiences are imprinted upon us, ready to be called up again when needed. We may not even be aware of all the old files that we have stored; some may be tucked away in the subconscious. But they're all there.

Society passes down a great deal of information from generation to generation. We are both the lucky benefactors and the unknowing victims of our common inheritance. A good deal of this information is very helpful. We no longer have to use the trial and error method to figure out which berries are edible, and which berries are poisonous. We are taught not to stand under a tree during a lightning storm, and we are taught to wash our hands before we eat. We are taught a great many useful things from our culture and our families.

We are also burdened with many things that are carried on simply because that's the way it has always been done. For example, much of the re-thinking of women's roles in society has had to overcome this rationale. This would be the very root of "consciousness raising": making conscious what is taken for granted. Making visible the blinders, curbs, and ceilings within our culture.

The family is the first source of such values and perceptions. What children see happening in the home will greatly affect their ideas about how things work. This is the yardstick (meterstick) they take with them into the world. The mature adult must be able to step back, and look at things anew, and see if they still make sense.

All of our schooling and intellectual development are part of the database passed on to us by society. We benefit from the labors of all the great thinkers, scientists, musicians, mathematicians, philosophers, and inventors who have come before us. As a result, students today have a tremendous amount of material to assimilate, including things like Calculus.

Having so much information available can be both a great treasure and a burden at the same time. I read a biography of Dr. Albert Einstein's life many years ago (*Einstein - The Life and Times*, by Ronald W. Clark). There's a discussion in the book concerning the extent to which Einstein's Theory of Relativity was founded on the works of his predecessors, and how much was due to his own internal inspiration. In truth, it was a combination of both. Einstein always recognized the debt he owed to his predecessors. In a speech to the

National Academy of Sciences, Einstein was quoted by the *New York Times* (April 26, 1921) as saying:

> The four men who laid the foundations of physics on which I have been able to construct my theory are Galileo, Newton, Maxwell, and Lorentz.

> In science... the work of the individual is so bound up with that of his scientific predecessors and contemporaries that it appears almost as an impersonal product of his generation.

Einstein threw nothing away, he took everything in, especially the failed experiments and unexplained physical phenomenon that seemed to violate Newton's Laws. An inherent skeptic, he was able to look at the body of work in the field, and by simply taking out one brick, by asking one question – "what if Newton's Laws are not complete?" – he was able to re-arrange the pieces of the puzzle to create a new picture of the relationship between energy, mass, time and space. Einstein combined an understanding of all the previous work with a fresh perspective, allowing him to look at things in a way they'd never been seen before.

Einstein took in the existing knowledge of physics, processed it in new ways, and ultimately expanded the body of knowledge. Einstein did very well by our tree standard.

This reminds me of another story. Every year, Beantown hosts a tournament for women's college teams. It was known as the "Mayor's Cup Tournament" for many years when it was still held in Boston. The event was eventually moved to central Massachusetts, and so is now known simply as the Beantown Tournament. Depending on the year, there may be twenty or more college sides entered.

It was many years ago, and the team was making the usual preparations for the tournament: getting T-shirts made, buying supplies, renting tents and equipment, setting up the brackets, and so on. I'll never forget how excited Betsy Kimball, our team president, was about this tournament. She really wanted the college students to be able to play some good rugby and have a good time that weekend. She brought so much enthusiasm to that event.

Now, Betsy was sort of the Methuselah of the team. She was a member of the original team when it was formed in 1976. She had been playing for some 15 years, or approximately 30 seasons, by that point in time, and had probably been involved with organizing and putting on any number of such tournaments and other events over the years. That's when it occurred to me. She acted as though this was the very first such tournament that Beantown had ever hosted. Betsy didn't consider this to be just another Beantown event; it was *this* year's Beantown Tournament.

The ability to focus and to be present to the moment carries over into everything. It's not just another day at the office; it's today. It's not just another kiss from your lover; it's this kiss. When you're playing a rugby game, you can't be thinking about last weekend's game, or the team you play next on the schedule. In fact, there's not even time within the game to gloat or brood over an especially good or bad play, because the game just keeps going on. You have to get right back up, and get where you need to be, and do what you need to do.

chapter 37
naked Olympics

The ability to focus on the present event is key to all athletics, but nowhere is it more essential than at the Olympics. Years of training, practice, sacrifice, and dedication all come down to one day, one race, one event. Even though I don't do a lot of winter sports (unless you include sledding, slipping, falling, and bread baking), I became pretty absorbed in the 1994 Winter Olympics. There was the Nancy-Tonya drama. And there was Bonnie Blair, hailing from my home state of Illinois, skating her heart out, and standing up for all that is good and Midwestern. And you had Picabo Street, Dan Jansen, Tommy Moe, and all the rest of the gang.

The athlete's story that stays in my mind, though, is Diann Roffe-Steinrotter, the "surprise" gold medalist in the women's Super-G event. (I won't even pretend to know that that is.) The day after her victory, newspapers across the country featured stories and interviews with Diann. Her quotes, printed in *The Boston Globe* (February 16, 1994) show that she, too, was skiing both weighted and naked. Here is how she described the Olympics in general:

The Olympics is just one day, one hill, 1 1/2 minutes in your life – whoever shakes and bakes the best out there is going to win it.

Naked. And yet weighted. Diann Roffe-Steinrotter was no novice at this sport. She had been up with early victories in her career as a teenager, and she had been down, even considering retirement in 1988. She took all of this with her to the 1994 Olympics:

I didn't have anyone to radio up and tell me what the course was like or what to expect; but when I inspected the course, my instincts and experience told me what to expect and how to ski it. I've inspected hundreds and hundreds of race-courses over 11 years, and that experience gives you something you can't get anywhere else.

Weighted. There's the old riddle: "What do you get when you don't get what you want?" The answer: experience. Diann had some of this sort of experience, too. One could ask why she decided *not* to retire after the knee surgery in 1986, and the disappointing season that followed. That's an answer that must have come from somewhere deep within. A decision, a belief in herself, the hope that things would get better, and the willingness to take the risk to see her dream through.

But then I was thinking, ski racing is the one thing I do better than most people in the world, and I kept pushing through. I had success in two stages of my career – very young when a lot of young racers were having success – and now. You can't put a price on experience.

Naked and weighted. Diann took with her both the wealth of past skiing experience to guide her tactical approach (weighted), as well as the realization that it was all about this one day, this one hill, and giving it her best shot (naked). There was more than this, though. Going into this competition, Diann was still grieving the loss of her friend, Ulrike Maier, an Austrian racer, who had died in a skiing accident just three weeks before the Olympics.

Ulrike and I were very close friends. Every time I step into my skis, I think about her. Her accident was just a matter of fate, but I think if she were up there today watching, she was saying to all the racers, 'Just point them downhill and go for it.'

Naked. It seems that we have two choices: to either cling to life, or to dance with it. The last chapter is the same in everyone's book. It's how you fill the pages in between. Life is about risks. Certainly, there are risks involved in letting go, and going for it. And yet there's another risk. The risk you take by *not* letting go.

What you miss risking, you risk missing.

chapter 38
go forward naked

In truth, naked and weighted is just another form of go forward, support. When you run forward with the ball, you're putting yourself out there. It's you against the world, or, at least the 15 members of the opposite team. On the one hand, you're vulnerable – you're the one everybody wants to tackle. But it's also exhilarating, too. Going forward involves a certain surrender to Serendipity and the unknown. Naked.

There are many forms of support in rugby. It's not just your teammates on the field and sideline, but also all the club history and resources: the field, the playbook, the alumni, and all the traditions that have been passed on. You don't play in a vacuum. When you play rugby, you are part of something much greater than just a gathering of individuals on any given day. Weighted.

chapter 39
naked and framed

Athletes are not the only ones who play naked and weighted. Artists are also caught up in this balancing act. Each time an artist starts a new piece of work, they stand there, naked, at the edge of a cliff. About to make something out of nothing; to give life to the insentient. The painter faces the blank canvas. The sculptor begins with common, raw materials – clay, metal, stone. The photographer puts in a fresh roll of film. The performer takes the stage. The musician begins with silence and a cold, inanimate instrument, and makes song come to life out of thin air. Writers start with the blank page.

There is nothing more terrifying than this, nor more exhilarating. Master songwriter Jimmy Webb ("By the Time I Get to Phoenix," "Galveston," "Wichita Lineman," etc.) described his take on the creative process in an interview with *USA Today* (April 25, 1995):

> The main qualifications for songwriting are 'having a soul like a piece of raw liver and a lack of inhibition. Songwriters say the things other people want to say. There's a nakedness to that.'

At the same time, the artist operates from within a particular frame of reference. The artist's works will be flavored by all the creative influences and life experiences that have shaped the artist's life. It is all there, at the tip of the pen or paintbrush, in the silence before the first note, and in the breath of the glassblower. An artist may be known for a few popular or striking pieces of work, but to understand the significance of a particular piece, one needs to look at it within the context of the artist's complete body of work. You can't know an artist by a single work. You have to look at all the different types of work they have created. Not everything will be marvelous and breathtaking, but it may be interesting. Much of it will be trial and error. What does an artist do, but create and grow? The artist is much like our tree. An artist who is not free to experiment, to fail as well as to flourish, will also never be free to play, grow or soar. They will be like the seed that refuses to sprout.

This discussion is bound to eventually trigger the question: What is art? I have a whole pocket full of answers, but the first thing I have to say is that art seems to be another one of those self-generating organisms. Like hope, if you think something is art – then it is art. This is not surprising, as the two – hope and art – are very closely related. And maybe the answer is again in the very act of asking the question.

I once got involved in a debate about the definition of art with a friend, who was an art history major. The question had come up in one of her classes. One theory held that art is a leisure time activity, as it is not essential to survival. People do not have the time or resources to devote to art until the basic needs – food, clothing, and shelter – have been secured. The fundamental assumption of this theory is that art is *not* a necessity. Does that mean to say that art is unnecessary?

The alternate theory considers art to be a vital human need, food for the soul. It's as necessary as breathing. It's a passion that wells up from within the person. When the cave people came home from slaying the woolly mammoth, they painted pictures of their prey on the walls of their cave. When early cultures developed pottery, they didn't simply make containers – they crafted pieces of art. It's not that one jug held water better than the other one; it was a matter of imbuing an object with some of the life of its maker, and deriving joy from the act of creating it, and using it everyday.

I tend to buy into the second theory, in that every individual has some sort of artistic impulses or leanings. Some of us wind up painting murals on chapel ceilings, and some of us color Easter eggs, sketch doodles on our desk calendar, refinish furniture, or hum made-up tunes. I sincerely believe that we are all artists in some sense.

If art is self-defining, then so is the title of artist. Believing will make it so. This brings back memories of the classic children's book, *The Velveteen Rabbit*, which tells the story of a stuffed toy rabbit who is so loved by a child that the toy turns into a real rabbit. Loving made it real. Believing can make it art.

chapter 40
pens and crayons

After reading an early version of this manuscript, my friend
Patty called me with some of her thoughts and comments.

"I really liked it," she said. "Of course, I might be biased,
since everything gets tied into rugby somehow. Well… Almost everything."

"What?"

"Everything gets tied into rugby, except for art. I mean, what
if you're not artistic? What if you can't draw or paint or write poetry?
I started feeling left out. I guess I feel like I'm more of a pen than a
crayon. And then I thought: Well, maybe my rugby *is* my art!"

But of course! What goes without saying almost *literally*
went without being said. The cliché, "poetry in motion," is as old
and worn out as it is still true.

Athletics and aesthetics have gone hand in hand since before
Greek and Roman days, in every culture and in countless and varying
ways. Sometimes sports are looked down upon as low culture.
Hockey and opera might seem to be completely opposite of each
other. But, what if they're really just at the far ends of a continuum?
Maybe they're not all that different after all.

To watch a well-played game of rugby is to truly witness performance art: the perfect mix of control and chaos, spontaneity and
discipline. Plays as carefully choreographed as ballet. The forward
pack synchronized in the scrum. And yet, enough improvisation to
match any jazz ensemble. Add chance, passion, commitment, honor,
and shear determination, and you have about all the ingredients for a
great rugby game. Shakespeare would be proud.

There has been much talk about emotional intelligence, and
computing an emotional quotient (EQ) to describe how well some-

one relates to people. One could also speak of a physical intelligence, or a kinesthetic quotient, to describe one's native physical aptitude. Some people, especially top-level athletes, seem to have far superior natural physical talents: body control, balance, vision, speed, and reaction times. Studies on NFL quarterbacks show that they perceive time to pass more slowly during the game, and so when they see a gap or a receiver, they seem to have more time to react to it.

What lifts athleticism to an art form? Creativity. It's not quite the same type of creativity that writes a poem, but it is still creativity. It involves a certain creativity to quickly evaluate game situations, recognize opportunities as they appear, and to make snap decisions in the midst of competition. It's a physical creativity that allows a player to read the field, identify a momentary window of opportunity, a hole in the other team's defense, with an overload here, and a support player coming up fast inside, ready to take the pass. What drives this creativity is the passion for the medium. Just as a singer loves to sing, a rugby player loves to play rugby. It's the transformation of our emotional energy into physical energy. It's about making something matter in our lives.

There are many other fields involving different types of creativity and media, which are also not given their due credit. For example, engineering is often maligned as a strictly plug-and-chug, calculation-crunching, linear-thinking profession. Whether you're an engineer designing computer systems, or a scientist trying to discover a little more about how the world works, creativity is involved. At its very core, creativity is about using all the tools available and finding new ways to do things. The difference is that engineers and scientists are most often concerned with finding an explanation for an external reality, a truth that is out there to be found. Artists, on the other hand, spend their lives trying to externalize their own personal internal truths into various physical media. Their art is the expression of what's inside them.

Einstein made an interesting observation about the role creativity played in his approach to his work. Speaking to his friend, Janos Plesch, he once said:

When I examine myself and my methods of thought I come to the conclusion that the gift of fantasy has meant more to me than my talent for absorbing positive knowledge.

(from *Janos: The Story of a Doctor*, by John Plesch)

When you think of Einstein, you might at first picture a chalkboard covered with calculations. But even Einstein – *especially* Einstein – relied on a child-like capacity for visualizing the fantastic, and setting his imagination loose to go play.

chapter 41
the paper clip

There is always something new to be seen in rugby, even if you've been playing for years, and you think you've already seen it all. The laws will change, and you'll start to see all sorts of new things. In the old days, for example, players could not be lifted up in a lineout. It was a penalty. Now it's allowed and it's standard practice.

I found a symbol of this concept many years ago, in a box of paper clips. I was doing some field work, and needed to wrap up some loose ends on the project, and so I'd gone to the site office on a Saturday morning. I had some paperwork that I needed to keep together, and so I reached into my box of paper clips, and pulled out something that should have been a paper clip, but it was not shaped like any paper clip I had ever seen before. It was missing the inner, small looped bend. It looked like just a rectangular-ish piece of wire. I quickly realized that this paper clip was not capable of clipping papers, and was essentially useless.

It occurred to me that I must have already used hundreds, indeed thousands of paper clips in my lifetime. And yet, I had never seen a paper clip that looked like this. Here was something so common and so simple, that I must have surely taken them for granted. Yet, there before my eyes sat something new that I'd never seen before.

Sometimes, it's easy to feel like saying, "What's left?" All the good stuff has already been discovered or written about already. There are only so many words in our vocabulary. Wouldn't a room full of monkeys with keyboards eventually put together every possible composition, from *The Bible* to *The Bridges of Madison County*? The key word there is eventually. Besides, animal rights activists would not allow such abuse to occur.

What this paper clip (which is not exactly a paper clip) says to me is that there's always something more to be seen, if we only look for it; more to be learned, more to be written, sung, played, or created. The onus is on us to be open to these discoveries. To have our eyes, ears, hearts, and minds open to new possibilities. To be naked.

I call this the "Lesson of Look." Look, and look again, as though looking at something you've never seen before. As if for the very first time. The usual can be extraordinary, if we only take the time to look.

I've heard it said that you could lock up an artist inside a very small jail cell, and even in the confines of this environment, they would still find art over and over again. As much as we are sensory beings, the vast amount of information to which we're exposed each day certainly far exceeds our capacity to absorb and process such information. What we see is just the tip of the proverbial iceberg of what we're exposed to. Another line from an Indigo Girls' song, "Love's Recovery," comes to mind: "I missed ten million miles of road I should have seen."

This line is particularly meaningful to me. I mess around with photography a little bit. When I lived in Illinois, one of my favorite things to do was to take pictures while I was driving. I know this sounds crazy, but the roads are very straight, and the land is flat, and so it really isn't as dangerous as it sounds. Obviously I don't use a very fancy camera. I take the term point-and-shoot quite literally. I never even look through the viewfinder.

I would get some very neat effects, though; from a soft focus to a complete blur. It makes the photos come out looking almost like paintings sometimes. There's nothing more eloquent than a shot of a lone tree standing out against a landscape of such profound flatness. And it's even better with the soft focus in the golden light of dawn or sunset.

Now that I live on the east coast, I don't do so much of this anymore. Driving around here is just too crazy. When people get inside their cars, it seems that they either forget or no longer care that there are other human beings out there in those cars. They forget how to be nice. They simply see other cars, not other people. We don't have to feel bad if we're rude to other cars, not as we would if we recognized that we were dealing with people. In the song, "One Of Us," Joan Osborne asks:

> What if God was one of us?
> Just a slob like one of us?
> Just a stranger on the bus, trying to make his way home.

I must say that this image evokes far more compassion than if she had said, "Just a stranger *in a car...*" In that case, I have a horrible feeling that the answer for many of us would be that we wouldn't treat him any more nicely than we treat all the other strangers in their cars.

And yet, we may interact with more people (cars) while driving around each day, than we do in any other area of our lives. I did a little experiment recently. While driving on the highway, I counted up how many cars (people) I interacted with over a certain distance. It wasn't even rush hour, but I found that I interacted with anywhere between twenty and forty people-cars over each five-mile span of road! And if I believe Brenda Ueland, there are gods and poets in each of those cars. It just seems that we have all become overly focused on the destination, and as a result, have little patience for, or interest in the road we have to travel along the way. A lot of people wouldn't mind missing ten million miles of road.

chapter 42
what is art again?

I'm not done answering this question yet. Driving in the Midwest is very different from driving the hills and valleys of New England. The Illinois roads run long and straight, with nary a curve or a hill to break up the ride. It's a very open, exposed landscape. You can literally see for miles in all directions.

When you're driving down a two-lane road out in the middle of Illinois, it's hard not to notice when another car is approaching from the opposite direction. In at least some parts of Illinois, the drivers have a curious custom of making a friendly wave to each other as they pass on these roads. I don't mean a big, hand-flapping type of wave. Rather, it involves just a slight lift of one hand, and a flick of the wrist, as it rests on the steering wheel.

I hypothesized that maybe this custom started because, in those parts, everybody knows everybody, and it's just safer to wave than to risk offending a friend, relative, or neighbor. I have driven quite a few miles of blacktop in Illinois, and it seemed to me that they didn't even have to know you or recognize your vehicle to wave. It was enough just that you were another human being traveling on the same road. It helped, though, if you were in a pickup truck.

Now, what does this have to do with art?

There is that split second, as your cars pass, and you're both giving that little wave, when you might actually make momentary eye contact with the other driver. For that split second, you recognize that there's another human being across from you. A face, a life, a whole history, within the metal, glass, and fiberglass. Not another car, but another *person*. And even though you've never met, in that crystalline moment, you are two people on the same road sharing some sort of human connection.

This, too, is art.

It's that moment as you're gazing at an image, or singing along with a song, or watching a play – and something connects with you. In some way, you understand a little part of "what is life?" as experienced by another person, and embodied in their creation. Something in what the artist created resonates with you. You've traveled similar roads. Art is communicating the human condition.

The song, "Closer to Fine," became one of my favorite songs from the very first time that I heard it. Why did that song grab me? Why did it grab half of America? Was it the rhythm, their guitars, their voices? Certainly these all contributed, but I think part of the answer is in the very first line, when the Indigo Girls sing, "I'm trying to tell you something about my life…" Think about that. What could possibly be a more basic, human, or profound appeal to make to another person? Isn't this what we're all about? Bouncing our voices, our very selves even, off of each other, to get some signal back that we're doing okay. We all seek affirmation and understanding. It is important to be heard.

It is likewise equally important that we listen. It is such a compelling need – the need to be listened to – that people will in fact pay $60, $75, $100 and more per hour to talk to a therapist. Think about it. What an unusual arrangement. One person talks (mostly), and the other person listens (mostly). It's not really about building a friendship; rather, it's a professional service. Of course, the therapist does more than just listen; asking the right questions and providing some perspective on things are also part of their job. But listening is a huge part of what therapists do.

Listening is a skill that everyone can practice and improve upon. The Lesson of Look also applies to people. In this context, it becomes the Lesson of Listen. Everyone has a story to tell, a very human story. And just when you think you've got someone figured out, they'll surprise you. There's always something more to be seen or understood about a person. It's just a matter of looking.

Art is a personal matter. What is deep and timeless to me may be silly and superficial to someone else. And vice versa. For example, I have this one photo that feels really special to me. It's called "a road not taken." It's a slightly blurred shot, looking up a road I was driving past, that rolls up and over the horizon, bordered by a field of soybeans, with a blurry stop sign in the foreground, telephone poles and a house in the background, and big, gray, brooding clouds hanging over it all. It was one of the first photos I ever had enlarged, and it's the image that I always go back to. I never tire of looking at it. There's something about the color of the sky on the horizon, a yellowish gray, and the road going off over the hill that always seems to pull me in toward that distant, unknown horizon.

Admittedly, there are some days on which I feel more connected with this photo than on others. Sometimes I see it, and sometimes I don't. And this is my own work. I think we all go through phases, though. Sometimes it is easy to see things, and sometimes we really have to work at it.

I think that a good relationship has much in common with a piece of great artwork, in the sense that you never tire of looking at it. Even though you've seen the Mona Lisa before, you keep going back because there is still something more to be seen in it. Her smile, the brushwork, the melding of colors. Some artwork may have flashy colors, or trendy subject matter, but does it have staying power? If you've seen it once, have you seen it enough? Great works of art – masterpieces – have depth and timelessness. Every time you look at them, you see them in a slightly different light. Maybe you also see something new in yourself in the process.

In a good relationship, we always need to be able to "see" the other person. Otherwise, we start taking people for granted. We may as well say, "I know all there is to know about you." We don't have to value the relationship and put energy into it, because it is already all that it is ever going to be. It has no potential.

People are full of surprises, and so are relationships. They're dynamic organisms. A great piece of artwork may inspire growth in the viewer, but a lasting relationship demands growth from both participants. Nobody rides off into the sunset for very long. It is a constant challenge and reward.

a road not taken (photo/rs)

Note, I didn't title it "*the* road not taken," partly out of respect for Robert Frost, but also because I don't believe there is only one road not taken. There are countless roads not taken, some of which we may be unaware, and this is just one of them.

chapter 43
can I have another potato chip?

This story comes to me second hand, so unfortunately I do not have a proper credit, reference, or footnote. A friend saw a comedian do this routine on TV many years ago, and she told me about it later. I've thought about it a lot over the years, and how it applies to relationships.

A guy is sitting in an easy chair, eating potato chips, and watching TV. His dog is sitting there, watching the bag of potato chips, and begging the way that dogs do.

"Can I have a potato chip?" the dog asks. The guy says, "No," and keeps eating his chips and watching the tube. About a minute goes by.

Again: "Can I have a potato chip?"

"No. I told you before. The answer is no." The dog sits there, watching the potato chip bag.

And again: "Can I have a potato chip?"

Finally, the guy gives in, and tosses the dog a potato chip. The dog eats the potato chip. The guy is watching TV again, and the dog is looking at him again.

"Can I have a potato chip?" the dog asks. The guy says, "What do you mean? I just gave you a potato chip!"

The dog says, "No. Not *that* potato chip. A different one."

When I tell people I think this story applies to relationships, I get mixed reactions. That is, some people see it the way I see it, and some people see it another way.

Some people think it's about having as many different "potato chips" as they can, if you get my drift, and I suppose that is also a perfectly valid interpretation if one wants to think about things that way. But, if that were the case, then the dog would have had a potato chip, followed by a Dorito, and then maybe a Frito, a Cheeto, and a Combo, and some Bugles, and so on.

The way I see it, a good relationship is... Always wanting another potato chip. Another kiss, another smile, another day together, another night together, another hug, another dance. With the same bag of potato chips. I mean person. It's about staying hungry. And hope-full.

Being hungry is a part of being naked and weighted, whether you're playing rugby, taking photographs, or courting a lover. Rugby always left me hungry. After every game, I'd recall the things that went so right, like a great scrum or lineout, and I just couldn't wait to get back out there and do it again. I would also recall the things that didn't go so well, like maybe the tackle that I missed or the play that I botched, and I'd crave the chance to go back out there and try it again. I think this is a big factor in why people play rugby for as long as they do. There's always something more to learn in rugby. There are so many variables: your teammates, the opposition, the field, the referee, the weather, and even the laws. There are constantly new opportunities to experiment with new strategies and techniques. There's always something new to be tried, and something new to be learned.

It's the same way with the arts. For example, I have all the photos that I've taken so far. Some have been enlarged, and many are in various stages of being matted and framed. And yet, as much as I love all of these photos, I am still hungry for the next good shot.

It is also possible to try too hard. Especially when you're a hungry person. It's when our trying gets in the way of our doing. It's when I try to get a really great shot that I have trouble taking any shots at all. Either I wind up shooting a bunch of junk, or I don't shoot anything at all, because I am afraid that it won't be great, and if it's not great, then it's not worth taking, right? Wrong again.

You can't force things. You need to balance the desire with an appreciation for the process itself. You need to be naked; open to whatever opportunities present themselves. What if you went into a rugby game intent on only one thing: putting pressure on their fly-half, let's say. Their scrumhalf is passing the ball out to the flyhalf, and you're in hot pursuit, but you don't even see that it was a bad pass. You could have picked off the pass and scored, but instead you tackled the flyhalf, who didn't even have the ball. You could miss an opportunity to score by focusing on just one element of the game, instead of playing the game with your eyes open.

Sometimes, I see a particular setting, and I think, "Now, there should be a good photo in that!" If I try and try and try to get that perfect shot – it never happens. I was working in New Jersey for a few weeks, and on the way to the site I saw a house with a nice tire swing hanging from a big, beautiful tree in the back yard, and some woods off in the distance. I was sure that there was a great photo there. I must have tried getting a good shot almost every day on my way to and from the site, and sometimes at lunchtime, too. I probably have a dozen pictures of that tire swing, and none worth looking at. I was trying too hard, and goodness only knows what else I missed along that stretch of road because I was so obsessed with that tire swing.

And then there are other times. I must have driven by the tree along Illinois Route 47 dozens of times, but I'd never given it any particular notice. But one time, one day, I saw it as I had never seen it before. Click. I got it. Just like that. Karma.

I believe in something like karma. It's about figuring out where you need to be at any given moment, and what you need to be doing there at that moment. You have to listen for it. The answer may not be apparent. Sometimes you have to go with your gut instincts. They're often right. We have to be like compass needles constantly trying to get into alignment with a dynamic, karmic, magnetic north. As we travel our various paths, our orientation with respect to north shifts, and we have to adjust. It's all about being attuned to what's going on around you, like a giant antenna, open and waiting to hear whatever might be coming through the airwaves. Or like a sponge, a filter feeder that takes in nourishment from everything that passes through it.

Karma is sometimes the only explanation for things. I don't believe in fate, but I do believe the soul may have certain leanings. As a tree seeks the sun, we gravitate to our callings. And we would do well to listen to them.

Solitude (photo/rs)

chapter 44
the moment (you've been waiting for)

Great artwork, ironically, is about both Timelessness and The Moment. Capturing the moment; the specifics of this day, these people, this place, this feeling. Think of all the pieces of artwork out there that do precisely this. Mona Lisa's smile. The Diner. All of Henri Cartier Bresson's work. And so on. We've heard it a million times. To understand the universal, one must understand the specific. The universe in a grain of sand. A blizzard in a single snowflake. And so on.

Some photographers work in the studio, carefully controlling the desired effects, to create on film what is held in their mind's eye. This is indeed a worthy craft. Digital technology has further enhanced photographer's ability to control and manipulate their medium. There is a whole other way to approach photography, though: in the field.

Prior to honing her craft as a writer, Eudora Welty's first full-time job was working as a publicity agent for the Mississippi office of the Public Works Progress Administration during the Depression. She toured the state, taking pictures, and writing stories for the local papers. Reflecting on this experience years later during a lecture series at Harvard University in 1983, she had the following to say about the craft of photography:

> With the accretion of years, the hundreds of photographs – life as I found it, all unposed – constitute a record of that desolate period; but most of what I learned for myself came right at the time and directly out of the *taking* of the pictures. The camera was a hand-held auxiliary of wanting-to-know.

It had more than information and accuracy to teach me. I learned in the doing how *ready* I had to be. Life doesn't hold still. A good snapshot stopped a moment from running away. Photography taught me that to be able to capture transience, by being ready to click the shutter at that crucial moment, was the greatest need I had. Making pictures of people in all sorts of situations, I learned that every feeling waits upon its gesture; and I had to be prepared to recognize this moment when I saw it.

I haven't taken many pictures of people, but I have a lot of photos of the Illinois landscape. And, I still enjoy taking spontaneous shots. These aren't carefully composed, perfectly focused pieces. I get a lot of misses: blurry, crooked, half-perfect shots. But, sometimes, by chance and good timing, I hit one right on. Chance, that the moment was there, and good timing, that I was there to see it. I don't have complete control over how the picture turns out. I've given up some of this control, and opened the door for Serendipity. This is not as easy as it sounds. It's about trusting what you can't see, and it may not even seem to make sense.

I often wish for things to be more clear-cut, black and white, and defined. Life for the most part, though, is lived in this gray zone. There are the questions that you pose to your therapist, and they give the only appropriate response possible: "That's the $64,000 question." That's when you know you're on your own. There's no guide, no book of solutions, no roadmap. Just the internal compass. There is only so much therapists can do. They can never get completely inside another person's head, mind, or heart. After all, there is what one will admit to family and friends, and there's what one will admit to a lover. There's what one will admit to a therapist, and there's what one will barely admit to oneself. It is hard to even know oneself sometimes.

chapter 45
ego

Every artistic endeavor involves a certain amount of risk. It's about putting yourself out there. In a sense, we are all artists, and our lives the objet d'art – the dynamic tapestries woven from one day into the next; the broad, swift brush strokes upon the canvas. As artists, we must trust and believe in ourselves, separate and aside from what the critics say. We're dealt our hands, and we play them out the best we can. We put ourselves out there everyday, with every card we lay down on the table.

I have a good friend, Marita Gootee, who is an art professor at Mississippi State University. I've known her for a while, and I've seen how she has inspired her students over the years, and I would have to say that she is someone who knows a lot about art. And people.

We were talking one time, many years back, about what it takes to be an artist. What she had to say surprised me at first. She said that, to be an artist, one must have a great ego. I questioned her, because it seemed to me that most of the artists I had encountered were pretty modest, humble, unassuming, and not overly self-centered, selfish, or arrogant in any way. She explained that artists must first and foremost believe in themselves, even when no one else does. They must continue to work on their art, with the realization that no one else may ever understand it, care about it, appreciate it, or see it as it was meant to be seen. This is why they need a great ego.

It makes sense then that some of the things perceived to be most egotistical also involve the greatest risks. For example, writing a book is a very egotistical thing to do. After all, who am I to think that I have something to say that anyone else wants to hear? But this is the writer's conceit, a necessary one for the trade. It's also a human conceit, necessary for living. It takes an ego to do anything, in the sense that you must always first and foremost believe in yourself, trust yourself, and believe that what you are doing is right and that it matters.

Many years ago, I had the opportunity to share a brief correspondence with an established author. I had been writing a column for the college student newspaper, and harbored some aspirations of being a writer, and so gave the author a few samples of my columns. In retrospect, it's not clear what I was looking for at the time. Perhaps I was hoping for some sort of blessing, or permission, or encouragement to pursue this calling. Someone to say, "yes, this is good enough."

Instead, the author had this to say:

I honestly have no advice for people who want to write. I wish I did. It's a very personal job and involves a lot of honesty. I think you alone can tell when you've written something that clicks, and when you've missed the mark.

The author confirmed what I had suspected all along: that you have to listen to what is inside of you. Some people will love you, some will hate you, and some will ignore you. But you have to do right by you. As I said, it is sometimes difficult to know oneself. But if you listen very carefully, you may find some inner truth. It is the Lesson of Listen applied to oneself. Honesty begins within. You're the only one who knows the cards you're holding.

The advice the author had to offer doesn't just apply to writing, though. It really applies to everything, if you think about it. It was ironic, the author's modesty: "I *honestly* have no advice…"

I had asked for directions; the author threw me a compass. I had been looking outside for a message, for a sign of approval, when all along I had the power within to give myself permission to follow my dreams, if I only listened closely enough. I was wearing the ruby slippers all along.

177

There's only so much someone else can tell you or give to you. You've got to figure things out on your own. I think I've said enough here. I've spent far too many hours in front of this computer screen, typing late into the early hours, all because I guess I thought I had something to share with you. I have said enough. I need to go out and play. And I encourage you to do the same. The world – it's a rough crowd out there sometimes. Do what you can to make it a nicer place.

Go forward, support!

chapter 46
from the poet in me to the poet in you

The Crayon Poem

I'd like to travel
the lifespan
of a crayon

all the hills and hollows
before that first pen

when lines were thick
and colors the rage

before the world
so black and white
became.

rs

Dear Rose!

Took your book and read it…

Comments:
Didn't know you ever rode a motorcycle!
When was this and why didn't you tell me?
D'oh – do you mean Duh?
When did you hurt your right shoulder?
Was this in rugby?
Why didn't you say you needed $20 for Tae Kwon Do?
I'm sure your book will be a bestseller.
We had a tire swing in Colorado – do you remember it?

Anyway – Congratulations – You've done a spectacular job.
When's the next one coming out?

Love,

Mom

References

Chamberlain, Tony. 1994. More US gold in them hills – Super(ior) performance helps Roffe strike it rich. *The Boston Globe*, February 16, 1994: p. 29.

Chamberlain, Tony, Powers, John, and from Associated Press. 1994. Roffe remembers Maier. *The Boston Globe*, February 16, 1994: p. 31.

Clark, Ronald W. 1984. *Einstein - The Life and Times*. New York: Avon Books.

Coppo, Richard. 2003. 1,905 US Rugby Clubs. *Rugby 2003 Directory - Yearbook*. Volume 29, No. 3 (April).

De Cervantes, Miguel Saavedra. *Don Quixote*.

Donnelly, P., and K. Young. 1985. Reproduction and transformation of cultural forms in sport: A contextual analysis of rugby. *International Review for the Sociology of Sport*, Volume 20, 1 - 2, p. 19-37.

Dunning, E., and K. Sheard. 1979. *Barbarians, Gentlemen and Players: A Sociological Study of the Development of Rugby Football*. New York: New York University Press.

Franken, Al. 1992. *I'm Good Enough, I'm Smart Enough, and Doggone It, People Like Me!* New York: Dell Publishing.

Frankl, Viktor E. 1959, 1992. *Man's Search for Meaning*. Boston: Beacon Press.

Goldberg, Natalie. 1986. *Writing Down the Bones*. Boston & London: Shambhala Publications, Inc.

Gundersen, Edna. 1997. Oprah, Tina bask in kinship, bliss on tour. *USA Today*, May 15, 1997: p. D1.

Hagerty, Edward. 1993. 1,377 US Rugby Clubs. *Rugby 1993 National Directory Issue*Volume 19, No. 1 (February): p. 1-2.

Seligman, Dr. Martin E. P 1990. *Learned Optinism.* New York: Random House.

Seligman, Dr. Martin E. P. 1993. *What You Can Change and What You Can't.* New York: Ballantine Books.

Sheard, K., and E. Dunning. 1973. The rugby football club as a type of "male preserve": Some sociological notes. *International Review of Sport Sociology*, Volume 8, 3 - 4, p. 5-24.

Ueland, Brenda. 1938. *If You Want to Write: A Book About Art, Independence, and Spirit.* Saint Paul, MN: Graywolf Press.

Vermes, Jean C. 1972. *The Girl's Book of Physical Fitness.* New York: Association Press.

Wheatley, Elizabeth. 1987. *A women's rugby subculture: Contesting on the "wild" side of the pitch.* Unpublished manuscript, University of Illinois, Urbana, Illinois.

Web Pages:
USA Rugby – www.usarugby.org
Rugby Magazine – www.rugbymag.com
Safety/Risk Management Information – www.epru.org
Beantown RFC – www.geocities.com/beantownrugby

Rugby and Soccer History:
www.rfu.com
www.soccerpulse.com
www.geocities.com/sissio/SOCCERHIST.html
www.geocities/tomokomatsui2002/history.html

Index

about the author

Rosemary Schmidt enjoys Early Grey tea, does not pack light, and avoids left turns wherever possible. She has spent most of her adult life trying to bulk up, and add some weight to her bird-like frame. She played rugby for the University of Illinois from 1986 to 1992, and for Beantown 1991 to 1995. She played hooker, and later flanker. Frankly, she wasn't great, she always scheduled too many away games, but she played with great tenacity, and brought good grub to the drink up. Just don't ask her to try to boat race. Unless it's for the opposite team!

about gainline press

Gainline Press was created in 1999, and is dedicated to publishing interesting books of significance. The name is derived from a common rugby term. Gainline is another term to describe the line of scrimmage. You usually start play from a scrum, lineout, or whatever, by first passing the ball out backwards. The ball may get passed back quite a distance before a ball carrier is able to run it forward. Sometimes the ball doesn't even make it back to where the play started, and so a typical comment might be, "Geez, they're not even making the gainline." The publishing business is very similar in that there is much work that must go into a book before there's anything to show for it. If you're holding this book now, you've helped me make the gainline. Thank you.

Gainline Press
PO Box 1166
Watertown, MA 02471
www.gainline.com